Journal
of
Beat
Studies

Volume 1, 2012

PACE UNIVERSITY PRESS • NEW YORK

Journal of Beat Studies

Volume 1, 2012

	vi	Letter from the Editors
Jimmy Fazzino	**1**	"A Trap Well-Enough Woven of Words": The Many Worlds of Brion Gysin's *The Process*
William Mohr	**23**	"Hard Blows of Love (Pick up on it like a horn, man, & blow)": Stuart Perkoff's "Round About Midnite" and Community Formation in Venice West
Tim Hunt	**49**	"Blow as Deep as You Want to Blow": Time, Textuality, and Jack Kerouac's Development of Spontaneous Prose

REVIEWS

Jonah Raskin	**89**	*Sutras & Bardos: Essays & Interviews on Allen Ginsberg, the Kerouac School, Anne Waldman, The Postbeat Poets & the New Demotics* by Jim Cohn.
Marc Olmsted	**92**	*East Hill Farm: Seasons with Allen Ginsberg* by Gordon Ball
Phil Dickinson	**95**	*The Cubalogues: Beat Writers in Revolutionary Havana* by Todd F. Tietchen

Phil Dickinson   100   *Capturing the Beat Moment: Cultural Politics and the Poetics of Presence* by Erik Mortensen

Ryan Ehmke   105   *Queer* (25th Anniversary Edition) by William S. Burroughs, edited with an introduction by Oliver Harris

Jonah Raskin   108   *Jack Kerouac and Allen Ginsberg: The Letters,* Bill Morgan and David Stanford, Ed.

Jennie Skerl   110   *Modern American Counter Writing: Beats, Outriders, Ethnics* by A. Robert Lee

William Lawlor   113   *Lawrence Ferlinghetti, 60 Anni di Pittura* (60 Years of Painting), Giada Diano and Elisa Polimeni, Ed.

Matt Theado   117   *Brother-Souls: John Clellon Holmes, Jack Kerouac, and the Beat Generation* by Ann Charters and Samuel Charters

Tom Pynn   120   *The Etiquette of Freedom: Gary Snyder, Jim Harrison, and* The Practice of the Wild, Paul Ebenkamp, Ed.

Matt Theado   123   *Be Always Converting, Be Always Converted: An American Poetics* by Rob Wilson, and *Beat Attitudes: On the Roads to Beatitude for Post-Beat Writers, Dharma Bums, and Cultural Activists* by Rob Sean Wilson

Penny Vlagopoulos   128   *Kerouac at Bat: Fantasy Sports and the King of the Beats* by Isaac Gewirtz

                         135   *The Beat Review* Index

Letter from the Editors

To our readers,

The *Journal of Beat Studies* is devoted exclusively to the scholarly criticism of Beat Generation writing and writers. Our mandate is to provide readers with intelligent and penetrating criticism across the range of Beat writing, including fiction, poetry, drama, autobiography, life writing, travel writing, and screenplay writing. The ultimate goal of the journal is to advance the quality of Beat Studies scholarship through application of diverse critical perspectives that address Beat production as both complex art and cultural critique. There has never been such a journal.

We are at a pivotal moment in the history of Beat Studies, one that provides an opportunity to reform practices in and philosophies of Beat scholarship over the last fifty years. Our mission is to model and stimulate paradigms of methodologically sound and critically innovative scholarly readings of Beat movement and associated writers. The journal accommodates interdisciplinary methodologies since Beat poetics and aesthetics did, and still do, promote border crossing. To those ends, we proudly offer in this inaugural volume essays that speak to this mission.

Tim Hunt's "'Blow As Deep As You Want To Blow': Time, Textuality, and Jack Kerouac's Development of Spontaneous Prose," based on archival documents consulted for the first time, foregrounds the emphasis on orality in Kerouac's mature compositional practices. In "A Trap Well-Enough Woven of Words": The Many Worlds of Brion Gysin's *The Process*, Jimmy Fazzino introduces an important early Beat novel, documenting its place in Beat transnational writing. William Mohr's "'Hard Blows of Love (Pick up on it like a horn, man, & blow)': Stuart Perkoff's 'Round About Midnite' and Community Formation in Venice West" attends to scholarly recognition of Stuart Perkoff's under-studied role in West Coast Beat jazz poetry. These works, by both established and new scholars, typify the kind of criticism that sustains and advances a vibrant field of scholarship.

The *Journal of Beat Studies* will always include reviews of new and significant scholarship. In this inaugural issue, we reprint a sampling of recent reviews from *The Beat Review*, the online publication of The Beat Studies Association. In future issues, we will present previously unpublished reviews of scholarly books treated at length by specialists in the relevant fields. Additionally, we plan to provide periodically a multi-review essay, which will survey and assess the state of the field of Beat Studies.

As long-time scholars of Beat literature, we have been painfully aware of resistance to the integration of Beat scholarship into canonical U.S. literary critical discourses. We hope that the *Journal of Beat Studies* will act as a counterforce to this resistance, clarifying the classic line of American writing staked in the nineteenth century and carried forward by Beat poetics even into the twenty-first. We undertake this project on behalf of Beat writers whose literary innovations continue to inspire readers around the world.

In closing, we wish to acknowledge and thank our colleagues on the executive board of The Beat Studies Association and members of the journal's editorial board for their unwavering support of and confidence in this endeavor.

Onward!

Ronna C. Johnson
Nancy M. Grace

"A Trap Well-Enough Woven of Words ": The Many Worlds of Brion Gysin's *The Process*

Jimmy Fazzino

British-Canadian writer, artist, and lifelong expatriate Brion Gysin is best known to Beat audiences as a one-time resident of 9 rue Gît-le-Coeur, the famed "Beat Hotel" that was occupied at various points by William S. Burroughs, Allen Ginsberg, Peter Orlovsky, Gregory Corso, Harold Norse, and other notables. There, Gysin and Burroughs pursued an intense collaboration leading to their joint development of the "cut-up method."[1] In "Cut-Ups Self-Explained" (1964), Gysin argues that "[w]riting is fifty years behind painting," a charge made all the more trenchant by the fact the Gysin was himself a prolific painter (*Back* 132).[2] During an earlier stay in Paris in the mid-1930s, there ostensibly to attend classes at the Sorbonne, he instead fell in with the Surrealist group in operation at the time. Gysin was invited to show his work at a group exhibition that included such luminaries as Picasso, Miró, Magritte, and Dalí, but he was devastated to find, on the day of the opening, his pictures being removed by order of André Breton on murky grounds of "insubordination" (Geiger 45). The same gallery would later hold a solo exhibition of Gysin's work, which was beginning to move away from overtly surrealist influences and would become increasingly complex and innovative over the next several decades. By the late 1950s at the Beat Hotel, Gysin was producing canvases that overlaid grid-like patterns with Eastern calligraphic scripts and sought to liberate language in ways analogous to his and Burroughs's cut-up experiments.

Jason Weiss has noted that Gysin's multi-genre, mixed-media approach to his work, which seems to vacillate or occupy a kind of middle ground between visual art and the written word, has led to both his unfortunate obscurity and his enduring significance "in this age when scholars and readers are eager to think across the disciplines, to find connections between cultures, to discern the underlying matrix of an artistic moment beyond fixed horizons of identity or traditional expectations" (*Back* ix). The hybrid identities (formal, linguistic, cultural, and otherwise) that Weiss views as central to Gysin's oeuvre are in many ways the obverse of a loss, even a refusal, of personal identity that becomes equally important to Gysin's mythos and worldview. He once confessed, "I have never accepted the color or texture of my oatmealy freckled skin: 'bad packaging' I thought. Certain traumatic experiences have made me conclude that at the moment of birth I was delivered to the wrong address"—adding: "I have done what I can to make up for this" (*Here* xvii). This last statement could apply to Gysin's incessant travels—a self-imposed exile or a pilgrimage with no known destination—and to the sum of his creative endeavors. His best-known work of fiction, his 1969 novel *The Process*, in which shifting identities and itineraries mirror the ceaselessly shifting sands of the Sahara, represents Gysin's most profound attempt at "making up" for the very fact of his birth.

The imaginative detours that cut a meandering path across Gysin's novel, however, not only "make up" for his birth but also contribute significantly to Beat discourses on race, gender, ethnicity, and religion as they offer an alternative, even a corrective, to familiar depictions of the "exotic" in Beat writing or the standard fare of what Brian T. Edwards has dubbed "hippie orientalism."[3] The cross-cultural aesthetics and wildly innovative narrative and figurative strategies that Gysin employs throughout the novel enable him to comment on racial and ethnic difference in a particularly complex and nuanced manner. The willingness of the novel's protagonist, Ulys O. Hanson, to "go native" in Morocco (where Gysin himself spent the better part of the 1950s after an initial invitation from Paul and Jane Bowles to join them at their Tangier villa) is perhaps unsettling at times, but a highly performative means of counteracting the relentless *othering* that has always been an orientalist hallmark.[4]

My central claim in this essay is that Gysin's novel is thoroughly *worlded* in scope and decidedly anti-orientalist in outlook, a claim grounded in a reading of the novel's understanding of personal identity and group affiliation as radically hybrid and mutable and yet firmly rooted in local soils and local histories, achieved in the novel through a highly wrought set of tropes and images revolving around the nexus of language and landscape. In using the terms *world* and *worlded*, I am indebted to *The Worlding Project: Doing Cultural Studies in the Era of Globalization*, edited by Rob Wilson and Christopher Connery who deploy the concept of the *world* as a critical term aimed squarely against forces of globalization and notions of "the global," seeking out the contingent and heterogeneous in opposition to the totalizing mechanisms of global capital and cultural hegemony. A *worlded* critical procedure will always be attuned to geographic and historical specificity and to material practices that run counter to the naturalized yet deracinated transcendence of the global.

In *The Process*, the linguistic and geographic permutations that become the most striking feature amount to nothing less than a vital "process" of postcolonial worldmaking. *The Process* is, in fact, a novel that contains *many* worlds. Changes in perspective, shifts in consciousness, and other like phenomena are consistently described in terms of leaving one "world" for another, and Gysin's novel demands a constant reorientation on the reader's part in order to account at each step for new horizons, new vistas, and a new relation to an immanent and heterogeneous totality. *The Process*, then, is an instructive example of *worlded* Beat writing, which, made radically expansive through its profound and paradoxical rootedness in space and time, runs counter to the deracinated transcendence of the global. From the margins of the Beat canon, Gysin points the way to an understanding of the Beats as deeply engaged with legacies of western imperialism and as prescient critics of Empire's new hegemony.

Gysin began composing the novel, his first, in 1965 and would spend the next several years in Tangier completing it (For an account of the novel's genesis and early reception, see Geier 201-229). The events detailed therein generally take place about a decade earlier, but it is a roman à clef only in the broadest sense. Gysin clearly had something more ambitious in mind, and his novel works on its source material in highly inventive and challenging ways. A long opening chapter introduces Ulys O. Hanson III, an African-American professor of history trekking through the Sahara in order to research his next book, which he plans to call "The Future of Slavery." To this end, Hanson has received funds from an obscure group called the "Foundation for Fundamental Findings," although he makes it only as far as Adrar, Algeria, before being turned back by French troops—"the Heavy Water Police" (67)—guarding the nuclear test site just to the south. The insidious presence of these and other agents of what Burroughs would call the "control society" permeates the desert, setting the tone for a series of uncertain crossings that structure Gysin's novel. Back in Tangier, having failed to reach "my Black Africa," Hanson is abruptly snatched away by Hamid, whom he calls his "Moroccan mock-guru" (6, 303). The two escape the violently escalating anticolonial unrest brewing in the city, fleeing to the home of Hamid's uncles, none other than the Master Musicians of Jajouka, based on the group of the same name introduced to Gysin by Paul Bowles. In 1954, Gysin opened the 1001 Nights restaurant in Tangier in order to showcase the Jajouka musicians, which in turn helped to introduce a wider audience to what is now called "world music."[5]

As Gysin's narrative grows increasingly fractured and hallucinatory, the demands of what the novel figures as "present time" begin to assert themselves more forcefully. For instance, Hanson meets the ghostly Thay Himmer, "last White Rajah-Bishop of the Farout Isles" (204), at a Tangier café, and it turns out that Thay and his wife, Mya, have been bankrolling Hanson through their Foundation for Fundamental Findings, meaning to embroil him in Mya's plot to take over the entire African continent. Hanson and Thay rendezvous with other members of the Himmers' organization at Mya's seaside citadel, Malamut, and when Hanson learns what the Himmers truly have in store for him, he is faced with a critical decision. The novel ends with one last set of narrative permutations (a watchword throughout) and a coda that returns us to a scene nearly identical to the opening chapter, leaving readers to ask whether this whole business has been, as Hanson suggests more than once, "a trap well-enough woven of words" (317).

Whether we agree that Paul Bowles' complaint to Ginsberg about the novel— that there is "an awful lot of naked Brion in there" (qtd. in Geiger 202)—is cause for disapprobation, Bowles does have a point. In spite of their obvious differences, Ulys Hanson can, and should, be read as Gysin's alter ego. Like Hanson, Gysin once wrote a book about the slave trade in Canada, and like Hanson, Gysin became one of the first "Fulbrighters" on the strength of that book.[6] Hanson's "mock-guru" Hamid is closely modeled on Moroccan painter Mohammed Hamri, who was instrumental in bringing the Jajouka musicians to Tangier and the 1001 Nights. The Himmers bear a strong resemblance to John and Mary Cooke, a wealthy American couple and early followers of Scientology. When Gysin became enmeshed in the Cookes' extravagant and tangled affairs in Morocco and Algeria, it ended up costing him his restaurant. This handful of major characters in *The Process* are least clothed in pseudonyms; "naked Brion" does indeed appear at various points in the novel, as when Gysin refers, by name, to a litany of former lovers.

Compelling though such personal revelations may be, they pale in comparison with the subtle (and not-so-subtle) ways in which the novel's immediate cultural and political context—in particular, the context of African decolonization—percolate through the book. There are references to the Algerian War and to the demonstrations and riots that erupted across Morocco in the run-up to independence, as well as to figures like anticolonial torchbearer Frantz Fanon, whose name in *The Process*, Francis-X. Fard—"world-famous psychiatrist and the internationally Prize-winning author of *Paleface and Ebony Mask*"(175)—also evokes not only Nation of Islam founder Wallace Muhammad Fard but also the Nation's most controversial former member. This recombinatory gesture on Gysin's part is typical of the author's method and has the effect of linking both Fanon and Fard to a larger history of Pan-Africanism and Black Power swirling around the novel. There are additional references to Senegalese poet-cum-president Léopold Sédar Senghor and his former Surrealist colleague Aimé Césaire, or "the Nabobs of Negritude" (181); to Claude Lévi-Strauss, aka "Professor Levy-Levant," leader of "the Paris school of social anthropology" (137-38);[7] and, for those more keen on waging a revolution of the *mind*, to psychedelic icons Aldous Huxley and Albert Hoffman (Mya's mentor, "Dr. Forbach of Basel") (221-22).

Along with these markers of its contemporary sociohistorical context, *The Process* weaves together a more remote, even mythic, history. Such is the tale of Hassan-i Sabbah and his band of eleventh-century Assassins. Readers of *The Yage Letters* will be familiar with Hassan-i Sabbah from Burroughs' final letter to Ginsberg, which announces, "'Nothing Is True. Everything Is Permitted.' Last Words of Hassan Sabbah The Old Man Of The Mountain" (Burroughs 70). The same letter equates Sabbah with Gysin and makes it clear that the imperatives of the newly developed cut-up method supersede Ginsberg's outmoded concern for his soul. The name "Assassins" is derived from the hashish rituals that adepts are alleged to have performed at Alamut, Persia (now Iran), their mountaintop fortress, and that inspired in turn the nineteenth-century *Club des Hashischins*, whose members included Charles Baudelaire, Théophile Gautier, and Gérard de Nerval. In *The Process*, the Assassins are figured as a loose-knit "Brotherhood" of mystics and ritual keef smokers whom Hanson seems to meet everywhere he goes. They are also closely associated with Hamid and the ritual performances of the Master Musicians, and their presence in the novel forms a circuit of reciprocity and mutual respect that exerts a countervailing pressure on the network of colonial authority following Hanson like a shadow across the desert.

In the end, the strength of Gysin's novel resides not in its verisimilitude but in its willful departure from any one version of reality, and *The Process* differs from many works of Beat fiction in its sheer narrative complexity, which entails no fewer than eight narrators and includes extensive transcriptions of tape recordings, journal entries, and computer files. The main narrative is threaded together with interstitial chapters by Hanson, but even his identity is multiple and grows increasingly elusive. Among whites and Europeans, he is Professor Ulys Hanson. To Hamid and other North African Berbers and Arabs, he is Hassan Merikani. Mya takes to calling him Ulysses-Hassan, and the Foundation for Fundamental Funds wants to name him "The Ghost of Ghoul" as they enlist him in the wild conspiracy that drives the novel to its conclusion. In effect, the novel describes a proliferation of identities that is also a *loss* of identity, and in the face of this personal and narrational slippage, *The Process* organizes itself mainly along geographical lines, with geography and identity becoming closely aligned; the opening paragraph makes these alignments clear and is worth quoting in full:

> I am out in the Sahara heading due south with each day of travel less sure of just who I am, where I am going or why. There must be some easier way to do it but this is the only way I know so, like a man drowning in a sea of sand, I struggle back into this body which has been given me for this trip across the Great Desert. "This desert," my celebrated colleague Ibn Khaldoun the Historian has written, "This desert is so long it can take a lifetime to go from one end to the other and a childhood to cross at its narrowest point." I made that narrow childhood crossing on another continent; out through hazardous tenement hallways and stickball games in the busy street; down American asphalt alleys to paved playgrounds; shuffling along Welfare waiting-lines into a maze of chain-store and subway turnstiles and, though them, onto a concrete campus in a cold gray whose skyscrapers stood up to stamp on me. It has been a long trail a-winding down here into this sunny but sandy Middle Passage of my life in Africa, along with the present party. Here, too, I may well lose my way for I can see that I am, wherever I am, out in the

middle of Nowhere when I slip back into this awakening flesh which fits me, of course, like a glove. (1-2)

One could easily imagine this scene cinematically. The narrator's voice-over accompanies the film's opening credits as a long aerial shot finds the tiny specks of a desert caravan. The camera slowly zooms in while the narrator recounts his "childhood crossing," which is itself set in terms of a bleak urban desert, until it fixes a close-up of Hanson as he "slips back into this awakening flesh." The motion of the camera would parallel the incessant motion of Hanson's childhood, described in formulations such as "out through," "down . . . to," "shuffling along . . . into," and so on. It would also foreground the thematics of movement and travel that shape the novel.

Considering the gap between author and narrator, a statement like the glib "It has been a long trail a-winding down here into this sunny but sandy Middle Passage of my life in Africa" may be off-putting, but it reflects the willfully flippant approach to language throughout the novel. The hackneyed image of something fitting "of course, like a glove," further belabored by its ironic self-awareness, suggests that the narrator goes about his figuration with at least some ambivalence. Perhaps it is entirely fitting that an African-American professor of the history of slavery would map out his own life in terms of a "Middle Passage"; Hanson's skin—and the question of embodied identity—remains a major preoccupation throughout the novel. The "Middle Passage" reference, coming as early as it does, evokes the opening lines of the *Inferno* as well: "Midway upon the journey [*nel mezzo del cammin*] of our life. . . ."; Hamid, then, becomes Hanson's Virgil. Like the name Ulys/Ulysses ("of Ithaca, N.Y."), the echoes of Dante, Homer, and Joyce reinforce, in splendidly ham-fisted fashion, the notion of Hanson as exile or wanderer.

But however self-reflexive and *constructed* Gysin's novel may be, none of this is meant to suggest that it bears no relation to a world outside of its own creation. *The Process* is firmly grounded in the world of history and politics, and unpacking its dense layers of reference and allusion is essential to this reading. For instance, the distance between author and narrator enables Gysin to imagine scenes that perhaps could not have been presented otherwise. A few years after the novel was published, Gysin reflected that despite all his years in Morocco his "lousy oatmeal skin" remained vulnerable to the sun, which posed problematic in terms of his identity: "When I'm with Africans, I forget that I'm white. But they can't forget it. I stick out like a sore thumb. From miles away across the deserts or mountains, I look like a colonial cop or a mercenary. Whose side am I on?" (*Back* 243). Based on these pronouncements, one can surmise that Hanson, black and able to "pass" as Muslim and African, fulfilled a deep-seated desire on Gysin's part to escape his "lousy oatmeal skin." In *The Process*, this idea of passing is thematized, with characteristic facetiousness, in regard to Hanson's career in academia. From his bath in Alger's posh Hotel Saint-Georges, he explains:

> I have taught: I have published. . . . My book could have made me a full professor; with tenure, what is more, in any good school in the East, and would have, I think, if I had only been white. As I ponder on this, I play with myself in the suds and stand up, creaming my body all over with soap in front of the full-length mirror. . . . When I applied for my Fulbright fellowship, I sent them this very white photograph of myself. When we all passed muster at a cocktail party before sailing, I thought some members of the board were surprised to see me in the old flesh, as we call it. . . . I laughed and saluted my white sponsors in the mirror, waving my cock at them all, before I rinsed off and became my black self again. (15)

The thematics of passing fit into a larger pattern of *disguise* and loss of identity in the novel. A few pages later, in a recognizable attempt at "going native" (a variation on passing), Hanson trades his "GI boots, field jacket and worn Levis for sandals, baggy *sarouel* pants . . . and this fine black burnous which has made [him] feel invisible, here, since it first dropped over [his] shoulders (21). From this point on, Hanson is largely assumed by others to be African and Muslim as he goes "more and more deeply disguised" (21). For instance, when he attempts to send a letter back to Fundamental Funds detailing his progress and need for more cash, he even "considered enclosing a street photographer's shot of [himself] taken in the thick of [Tangier's] Socco Chico crush and scrawling across it, perhaps: *'Which one is me?'* " (121).

Hanson remains the protagonist throughout, but each chapter of Gysin's sprawling novel is narrated by a different character (Hamid, Thay, Mya, several of Mya's associates and operatives) and becomes a world unto itself—complete with its own history, its own language, its own point of view, in effect creating the novel's polyvocal desire to thematize and to interrogate the very process of subject formation. Chapter titles such as "I" and "Thou," "He" and "She," "You (Fem.)" and "You (Masc.)" are a first clue to this effect. Then, too, the narration of illiterate Hamid is recorded "almost by accident" (81) on Hanson's prized Uher reel-to-reel (a favorite of Gysin's as well). Like Hanson, Hamid is adept at passing between worlds, and when he recounts his youth in Tangier as a streetwise hustler and smuggler, it stands in sharp contrast to the idyllic scenes of time spent with his Master Musician uncles in the hills of Jajouka. But the centerpiece of Hamid's narration is his depiction of the mysterious Bou Jeloud festival, which Bowles had first taken Gysin to see in the early 1950s and in which Gysin recognized the same Dionysian energies as those that had once animated the ancient Rites of Pan. The next long chapter, narrated by "Cheshire Cat" Thay Himmer, provides an account of the burgeoning subculture within Tangier's expatriate scene that, with its distinctive mix of spirituality and hedonism, presages the later influx of "hippie orientalists" inspired in large measure by the presence of Gysin, Burroughs, and Bowles.

Significantly, however, especially in terms of the phallocentric Beat subject, is Mya Himmer's narration, which serves as an important corrective to the male characters that make up the first half of the novel. Distinguished by a rush of ellipses and italics which is extemporaneous and performative and looks typically "Beat" on the page, Mya's narrative presents a distinctly different history of events particularly in the account of her Native American upbringing in Canada, surrounded by strong women and the magic of storytelling. In Mya's chapter—and in the final sections of the novel, which involve increasingly experimental narrative tactics (e.g., fragments from a journal, a transcribed computer archive, and a pair of chapters from the Africanus twins, brother and sister who speak to and for one another as they merge voices and even sexes)—we discern a strategy to give voice to the Other, whether figured in terms of gender, race, indigeneity, or, finally, as blurring the line between human and non-human (e.g., the tape recorder, the computer).

This highly fraught enterprise is recognized as such in the novel and made visible through its seemingly endless succession of revisions and reversals that, in conjunction with the relatively small cast of characters, manage to create the illusion of vast space in what turns out to be a rather hermetic, self-contained textual universe. One set of verbal and *tactile* formulas favored by Hanson deals precisely with this idea of a world in miniature and thematizes the correspondences between "big world" (the world *out there*) and "small world" (his own private world). Significantly, this pattern marks the the opening scene of the novel in which Hanson is able to "slip back into" himself by performing the detailed, well-practiced ritual of fitting his keef pipe together, filling it with keef (the "green passport" Hamid has given him), and lighting it: "I make these moves," he explains, "not just out of habit but with a certain conscious cunning through which I ever-so slowly reconstruct myself in the middle of your continuum; inserting myself back into this flesh which is the visible pattern of Me" (3). This meticulous process, which recurs throughout the novel, is described in terms of an intimate connection Hanson shares with the objects he manipulates. The match and matchbox are limned in especially vivid detail: "Each match is a neat twist of brown paper like a stick dipped in wax, with a helmet-shaped turquoise-blue head made to strike on the miniature Sahara of sandpaper slapped onto one side of the box" (3). Calling the strip of sandpaper a "miniature Sahara" is not simply a clever bit of wordplay. It becomes a reversal of the synecdochic relationship in *The Process* between desert and world, whereby an object in Hanson's immediate consciousness stands in for the desert as whole and renders it legible in its totality.

The matchbox, however, still contains a profound mystery that gets at the core of how language functions as constitutive of both self-perception and objective reality—a major concern of Gysin's novel. As Hanson recounts:

> I know this whole business is a trap which may well be woven of nothing but words, so I joggle the miniature matchbox I hold in my hand and these masterpiece matches in here chuckle back what has always sounded to me like a word but a word which I cannot quite catch. It could be a rattling Arabic word but my grasp of Arabic is not all that good and no one, not even Hamid, will tell me what the matches say to the box. . . . If I remember correctly, Basilides . . . reduced all the Names proposed by the Gnostics into one single rolling, cacophonic, cyclical word that might well provide a Key to the heavens: "*Kaulakaulakaulakaulakau...*" Can the matches match that? (3)

What Hanson means by "this whole business" is not yet clear in these opening pages, but it most immediately refers to his elusive sense of self. He plays ceaselessly on the homology of *word* and *world*, and as the narrative takes shape, one begins to suspect that the "trap woven of words" refers to the novel itself. This early passage also raises important issues of communication, of the ability or inability of various characters to communicate with each other, with the landscape, and so on. These appear with increasing frequency as the novel progresses, crystallizing in events such as Hanson's difficulties translating and transcribing his various narrators; in Thay and Mya's occult study of "grammatology"; in Thay's subsequent vow of silence; in Freeky Fard's brother, Amos Africanus, his tongue mutilated at the hands of French colonial troops; and other equally resonant instances.

Most significant in the above passage is Hanson's reference to the Egyptian Gnostic Basilides, whose cyclical word "*Kaulakaula . . .*" foreshadows the act of permutation which becomes the novel's central conceit and plot device. The *zikr*, or ritual recitation of the names and attributes of God (*Allahu Akbar, Subhan'Allah, La ilaha ilallah*), is depicted at several points in the novel—with Hanson and the "Assassins," with Thay and the Hamadcha Sufi brotherhood—and in Thay's final exhortation to Hanson that he "permutate the *zikr*" (187), which Hanson accomplishes in truly postmodern fashion with splices and loops on his reel-to-reel tape recorder. It is the climactic event upon which the entire narrative hinges. The act of *permutation* thus becomes a dominant trope in *The Process*, and just as Sufi initiates cycle through the many names of God, Gysin's novel cycles through its various narrators, tropes, and language games.

Allegorical permutation in the realms of history and politics—especially in relation to colonial history and postcolonial politics—is a tactic that gives *The*

Process much of its critical charge. The novel's polyvalent allegories allow untold stories and marginalized voices to be heard in all their unsettling complexity. We learn, for example, that Mya was born Jackie Mae Bear Foot, a Native American princess, lending a degree of gravitas and historical significance to her otherwise monomaniacal and seemingly capricious plan to take over Africa—perhaps now on behalf of all the world's dispossessed, of those victimized by all forms of colonialism. The novel offers no easy answers to Mya's motives, yet it complicates them enough for us to imagine multiple possibilities. Mya's chapter also recalls a poignant scene of indigenous female knowledge and community—a world unto itself. She remembers that "[i]n winter, it could be sixty degrees below zero . . . Fahrenheit, of course . . . and we'd all sit in the kitchen in front of the fire . . . all my grannies and me . . . and we'd wait for the mushroom tea to work and, when it did, why it was *true!* . . . we used to simply *fly* away to another land that all those poor white people outside . . . those palefaces, never knew" (217, italics and ellipses in the original). Mya continues, "Home was another world. We were seven generations of women . . . believe it or not [. . . .] There were no men of *any* kind around our house . . . *ever*. Greatest Granny, as I called her, insisted that men were bad for the mushrooms . . . and she knew *all* about *them*. Dream-mushrooms always came up out of the ground when she called them by name" (218). This scene, and the magic it contains, provides an antidote to the patriarchal knowledge proffered to Mya by one Aldous Huxley, and with its claim that "men were bad for mushrooms," the wisdom of Mya's grandmother neatly reverses the usual shamanic line that women's magic is sure to spoil a spell or potion.

By presenting the concept of "Borbor" as a potent magic and a "mysterious substance" (146) that allows women such as Mya, who calls herself Calypso, to control the men around them, the novel plays with the verbal slippage between Borbor and "bourbon" on more than one occasion, effecting Gysin's keen negotiations of language, gender, and religion. Even Burroughs, for example, understood Mya and her Borbor to lie at the heart of Gysin's novel, writing that "the basic message of the book is too disquieting to receive wide acceptance as yet . . . for the book is concerned with rubbing out the word as the instrument of female illusion. The Himmer empire is based on the use of Bor-Bor, the drug of female illusion" (qtd. in Geiger 201). Burroughs himself may be "disquieted," but we can discern, especially in Gysin's rendering of Mya's childhood, a fascination with and respect for female empowerment that goes beyond anything in Burroughs' corpus.

A fascinating example of such empowerment is the fact that it is also from Mya that we learn Thay's history, which turns out to be a revision of the "white god myth," positing an anti-orientalized East that is dynamic, multiple, and modern. Mya tells Hanson, "I'm sure you think you know the rest of the story . . . but, *no!* The Himmers were different. In the next generation, the family went native to conform with some local prophecy which allowed them to crown themselves rajahs with full native pomp" (205). Mya's overall depiction of Thay's upbringing provides an image of a post-colonial network oriented away from the United States and toward an autonomous and heterogeneous Pacific Rim:

> [T]he Himmers were always *very much* of the East. They shopped in Singapore instead of San Francisco, for example . . . things like that. Black sheep of the family, like Thay's queer Uncle Willy, fled to Hong Kong and Macao before settling down on a remittance in some super-civilized place like Peking. Girls of the family were rather more spartan. They ran away to spin in an ashram in India with Gandhi . . . or took vows as Buddhist nuns at the court of the Queen of Siam. (205)

Like her provocation—*you think you know the rest of the story*—this is a history that reminds us that colonial histories are as contingent as they are mutable, an idea reinforced by Gysin's overall strategy of narrative fragmentation and by the final incommensurability of the novel's many points of view.

Verbal transmutations such as "Borbor/bourbon" and especially "word/world" point to profound correspondences between language and landscape in *The Process*. One possible referent of the titular *process* is the ceaseless transformations of the Sahara's substance as rocky plains of "reg" become sandy "erg," great dunes that in turn proceed to "'colonize' broad expanses of flat *reg*" (318). Portraying the desert as dynamic, as a living, breathing, speaking organism, is a major impulse in *The Process*. The "landscape as body" metaphor could certainly fit in with the kind of shopworn figuration that Gysin seems to revel in, although we can read something more significant here as well. Much of this trope has to do with *reading* the landscape, making a potentially threatening or alienating place more legible. Hanson is able to "slip back into" himself with the hypersensitive manipulation of his *own* body and relationship with the "miniature Sahara of sandpaper" on his "masterpiece matchbox" (2-3). Farther along, his desert caravan looks into the "watering eye of the mirage" which is "the great Show of the World" (47).

In extension, this conceit signals the novel's overall strategy of depicting geographic space through a process of imaginative mapping and remapping. Hanson, for example, had tried to convince his friend Hamid to be his guide into the Sahara, but it was Hamid who required "a bout of instruction in the map" (9). Spreading out a map of the North African Maghreb, Hanson explains it in corporeal terms to Hamid: "On this map, one handspan to the right along the Mediterranean shore lies Woran. With your thumb on Woran, your little-finger lands on Algut. If you pivot due south from that white city on the cliffs, your thumb will fall on Ghardaïa, the mysterious desert capital of the Dissident Mozabites" (9). But as always, the mapping process is fraught with the danger of illegibility, of losing one's way: "The trouble with this map is that it has two big insets of Woran and Algut . . . and these effectively obscure the desert trails to the south" (9). Hamid, mostly bemused by Hanson's entire project, reads his own meaning in the map:

> He pointed out that the Great Desert is in the shape of a camel stretching its neck right across Africa. . . . He laughed like a lunatic to see that the western butt-end of his camel was dropping its Mauretanian crud on the Black Senegalese. . . . The head of Hamid's camel drinks its fill in the sweet waters of the Nile. The eye of the camel, naturally enough, is that fabled city of Masr, where the Arab movies are made and all the radios ring out over streets paved with gold. Us poor Nazarenes call the place Cairo, for short. (9)

Hamid's benighted attitudes toward the "Black Senegalese" and "poor Nazarenes" also fit into a larger pattern of reversal in the novel—a friend of Hamid's, for example, asks the telling question, "why can't [Hanson] be a Muslim like everyone else in the world?" (86)— and function not so much to elicit our censure as to turn the tables on the Christian west and its own universalizing rhetoric.

Depicting a landscape that bears the inscriptions of history is an essential component of *worlded* geographies in Beat writing and elsewhere. The orbit of Gysin's novel includes textual assemblages such as Antonin Artaud's *Voyage to the Land of the Tarahumara*, in which Artaud's paranoiac-anthropological methods drive him to read the Central American landscape palimpsestically, to unearth, from beneath the accreted layers of western civilization, signs of an indigenous culture nearly destroyed by European colonialism and Mexican nationalism in turn. *Tarahumara*, like his earlier manifestoes for the "Theatre of Cruelty," is a fiercely anticolonial text, and echoes of Artaud can be found in such disparate Beat writings as Burroughs and Ginsberg's *Yage Letters*, Philip Lamantia's posthumously published *Tau*, and Amiri Baraka "Revolutionary Theatre" manifesto, which takes Artaud's imagined play *The Conquest of Mexico* as starting point for his notoriously confrontational Black Arts aesthetic.

Likewise, *The Process*'s discourse on race and religion is characterized by an awareness of geographic and historical contingencies. For example, describing a building style he likes to call "Sudanese Flamboyant" (28, 51), Hanson explains that it is "Mesopotamian in origin, surely, linking this desert with that other called Arabia Felix—not called Felix because happy but because it lies *al limine* (the Yemen), to the lucky right hand when you look back east across the Tigris and the Euphrates, east to the Gobi from whence all the palefaced freaklinas of history have always swept down on us poor Africans" (66-67). Hanson's evocative descriptions present a worlded vision of connection and collectivity in the face of colonial oppression. A common substance and a common history "link" the Sahara and its inhabitants with far-off places and peoples. The novel repeatedly raises such questions of the meaning and status of various racial, ethnic and cultural identities (e.g., Muslim, Arab, Berber, African, black, white, Christian, European, American) and, in particular, Hanson's identity in the eyes of his interlocutors. For his part, Hanson casts a wide net in asserting a shared community of all Africans, whereby what is lost in the strategic erasure of difference among Africans is gained in the assertion of a shared history and dedication to a common cause, although the novel is at pains to show diverse, often incommensurable, visions of a united Africa.

As a worlded text, Gysin's novel is committed to, and organized around, apprehensions of a "world-horizon" much like the one Rob Wilson presents in *The Worlding Project*, in which he speaks of a "world-horizon" brought near, made "local and informed, situated, instantiated as an uneven, incomplete material process" (212). We see this philosophy manifested in Hanson as he prepares to meet for the first time with representatives from the Foundation for Fundamental Findings: he muses, "One thing I forgot to tell the Foundation when I applied is that I have left not one foot back in *their world*, as they think, but a mere fading footprint. This foot I have put forward into the Sahara is already firmly implanted in *this African world*, where my guide so far has been Hamid" (17, emphasis added). Farther into the desert, he states that "here on the desert as out on the sea, the round swell of the Earth is your rise in the road. . . . The watering eye of the mirage is the great Show of the World. On its dazzling screen you assist at the creation and destruction of the world in flames" (47). Even farther into his journey, Hanson reaches the shrine of Hassan-i Sabbah with its elaborately decorated mosaic floor, which as he reflects upon their swirling colors become a vehicle whereby "[y]ou step from this world into a garden and the garden is You" (61). The will to transcendence implied in Hanson's world-visions is strategically undercut by the baroque profusion of these tiles (as it is by other characters' narration as well), and in effect, Hanson's shifting perceptions of the world and his place in it reflect Wilson's understanding that the intimation of immanence and material becoming stands in opposition to the totalizing homogeneity—belied by the commodity spectacle's multifarious falsity—of globalization and the global.

It should not come as a surprise, then, that in the worlded multiplicity of *The Process* the world itself emerges as a powerful organizing trope and topos. Thay Himmer, for example, describes his initiation into the Hamadcha brotherhood as "land[ing] in a new world" (138). Leaving the Medina for the Socco Chico is like "leaving one world for another" (140), and Thay later states, "Living between two worlds, as I did, I got provoked by Mya into doing the one thing one should never do—introduce one world to the other" (152). Sometimes, Africa and the Sahara are synecdochically connected to "the world," as when Mya tells Hanson, "We would both be happy if you would accept to come with us to 'Malamut' [her desert fortress] . . . where we have some great plans under way . . . for Africa . . . for the world" (233, ellipses in the original). Fard's wife and one of Mya's associates, Affrica "Freeky" Fard (née Africanus), writes in her journal about the desert's "hostile" fauna: "They would contend, I suppose, that they fight for water but I see their innate hostility as just one more example of the extreme nature of the Sahara; of the world" (286). Finally, internal and external worlds are linked metonymically in the figure of the *market*. For instance, a train conductor with whom Hanson shares his keef tells him, "Beyond this town [Bogdour] lies Oujda and the border. If you have no baggage [Hanson has none] you can easily go around it. The World is a Market" (72). And soon afterward, Hamid tells him, "We say about people like you: He can walk in the *souk* of my head, the marketplace all Arabs live in" (82). One of the many affinities between Gysin's and Burroughs's work is this shared image of the market. In a crucial sequence from *Yage Letters*, reprised in *Naked Lunch*, Burroughs writes of a "Composite City where all human potentials are spread out in a vast silent market" (50). For both writers, the market becomes a potent symbol of hybrid exchange and the liberatory promise of radically proliferating desires.

In topographical terms, however, the world that Hanson and the others most often confront is a desert, as noted above, yet when we might reasonably expect the desert to be presented as a void place: barren, unchanging, inscrutable—in short, orientalized—*The Process* presents the desert as full of dynamism and energy, marked by history, and eminently legible. Hanson and other characters are able to "read" the desert at every turn. This is not to say the "voice" of the desert is always benevolent. Often, it is the voice of Ghoul, "the Djinn of the Desert, Keeper of the Land of Fear" (6), who leads travelers astray and to madness and death. Other times, however, the voice of the Sahara consists of the "sibilant" sounds of its inhabitants. As Hanson explains:

> When desert-dwellers meet, they stand off a few paces to whisper sibilant litanies of ritual greeting, almost indistinguishable in sound from the rustling of stiff cloth, as they bare a long arm to reach out and softly stroke palms. They exchange long litanies of names interwoven with news and blessings until a spell of loosely knit identity is thrown over all the generations of the faithful like a cloak. . . .
>
> Everything crackles with static electricity as if one were shuffling over a great rug. Everyone in the Sahara is very aware; tuned-in to the great humming silence. (22)

This poignant image evokes a deep resonance between the "desert-dwellers" and the landscape they inhabit. A hostile place is made hospitable by their rituals and the communities those rituals create and sustain.

Hanson is sensitive to the "voice of the desert" from the outset, but a more complete immersion in its landscape and a corresponding diminution of his identity as American, even as human, are required for a more profound participation to occur. At several points, Hanson likens himself or another to the "winsome jerboa" or to the fennec, "that odd desert fox" who hunts him—"My ears are . . . bristly antennae that pick up and tingle with the silky sound of the sand sighing across the Sahara" (120)—in another set of formulas that indicate, with ritual repetition, a renewed ability to apprehend the vibrations and energies suffusing the Sahara. Waiting outside in the rain at a desolate train station early in the novel, Hanson hears "ranked choruses of bullfrogs recit[ing] the interminable Word they were set a long time ago, now, as their *zikr*: '*Kaulakaulakaulakaulakaulakau . . .*'" while "bats looped about the lamps they lit along the track, presently: '*Train coming!*' The bats squealed up into their ultra-sonic frequencies like the brakes set on distant steel wheels" (12). These are not instances of mere anthropomorphism but rather an initiation into deeper mysteries that exceed classification. Language and landscape, sense and signification work together in complex and unexpected ways to convey a singularly performative conception of community that pulls together the individual and his or her environment, native and foreigner, human and non-human, language and the ineffable.

It is the Brotherhood of the Assassins, however, that becomes the prime exemplar of the novel's desert vision of subterranean community and connectivity. The loose-knit community of Assassins, which refers to the eleventh-century cult of Hassan-i Sabbah, conjures a long history of transgression and intrigue. The exact nature and status of their Brotherhood is hard to pin down at any point in the novel, but this is likely by design, and upon his first night spent in their company and sharing in their rituals, Hanson has this strange revelation: "There is no friendship: there is no love. The desert knows only allies and accomplices. The heart, here, is all in the very moment. Everything is bump and flow; meet and good-by. Only the Brotherhood of Assassins ensures ritual continuity, if that is what you want and some do; for the lesson our *zikr* teaches is this: *There are no Brothers*" (35-36, emphasis in the original). All of this may appear far too insular or esoteric to have any real bearing on a world outside the text's own making, and with characteristic shrewdness, *The Process* seems to endorse exactly such a conclusion: Near the end, in a supremely self-reflexive gesture, Hanson once again muses that "this whole business is, of course, just a trap well-enough woven of words" (317). Yet nothing could be further from the truth. Despite Hanson's demurrals, the novel is never merely a formal exercise, and certainly not, as John Geiger asserts, "a cut-up of memory and pure invention" (28). In his usual cryptic manner, Hamid often tells Hanson, "We are all Assassins," and it is as if the Brotherhood must be created anew with each performance of its rituals, just as new worlds are created in the novel with each permutation of the Word. It is entirely possible, then, to read the novel—especially its latter sections, where Mya's plans "for Africa . . . for the world" unfold and then unravel—as nothing less than Gysin's postcolonial critique committed to demonstrating the relationship between geographic and historical emplacement and interpersonal connection.

Shifting from the spatial to the temporal aspects of the relation between self and other, we could say that *worlded time* exceeds, but must also account for, historical time. Accordingly, one of the most pressing, if often submerged, concerns of Gysin's novel is how to represent the folds of worlded immanence extant within the structures of "present time," that is, historical time. Another way of asking the question is where—and what exactly—is *history* in Gysin's novel? In *The Process*, "present time" most often refers to Mya Himmer's plans "for Africa . . . for the world," which, as the novel progresses, we begin to understand are a response to and even a continuation of the Moroccan independence movement and subsequent resistance movements in North Africa. One "phase" of the Himmers' plot is to free members of the "First Revolutionary Government," including Ben Baraka, in exile at "Fort Tam." The presence of Fard/Fanon among them suggests broader Black Nationalist or Third World Marxist ambitions. Thay and Mya continually beseech Hanson to "snap into Present Time" and assume the role of "The Ghoul," leader of their new Africa, which is to say that, for the Himmers, Hanson's usual keef fog obscures the present moment and would only be a hindrance to their designs. But there is much in Gysin's novel to suggest that keef, and its corresponding "keef time," is the name for another, more radical conception of history and politics. For instance, as Mya's officers make their way from Tam to the final rendezvous at Malamut, "present time" and "keef time" seem to converge in a series of increasingly bizarre locations and occurrences—highly ambivalent scenes that are tightly bound up with North African history and politics. The ruins of the recent colonial past have been occupied by newer, more dubious forces, a shabby amalgamation of imperialist vestiges, Marxism, and Arab Nationalism; at Tam, which has the appearance of "a tiny, crenellated white toy fort" (267), the Himmers' secretary, Olav, reports the following:

> We have all been quartered in the Officers' Mess, which was obviously built back in colonial days. Nearby, another unlikely relic lies awash in the sands. It is a long building in concrete built in the form of a transatlantic tanker and is said to have been a brothel whose rooms were the cabins in the superstructure. Theirs was a bar in the captain's bridge. The well-deck

> was a swimming pool surrounded by walls like the prow of a ship. Today,
> this astonishing structure has the Cuban flag painted on its side. (268)

The beached whale of European imperialism lies exposed and desiccated, and history repeats itself as farce as the travelers are questioned by a bearded captain dressed like Fidel Castro. The brothel in the form of an oil tanker is an unambiguous metaphor for colonial exploitation, while the Cuban flag now painted on its side points to a very real history of third-world solidarity.

Yet there is also something rather pathetic about the second-hand nature of the iconography and perhaps even the cause, which the novel exploits as a critique of dying colonialism, to use Fanon's very apt term. The party, for instance, as it leaves Tam, catches a ride atop "a cargo of mattresses" and are driven to the coast, where Olav continues:

> We are in the newly ruined Spanish capital city which must once have been shining white; perhaps, only a year ago. Unless someone catches this place pretty quick, it is going back to the desert. Only the barracks are well kept, while private houses and the hotel have been boarded up or have already fallen into ruin since they were broken into and looted. A few Arab fishermen in anonymous rags slouch through the streets and along the abandoned *avenidas* of shut shops. I noticed them hanging their nets from the marquee of a dilapidated movie house down by the beach. (269)

The ruined capital becomes a lesson to the well-kept barracks. The nationalist officers, like the captain in Tam with the Castro beard, are using borrowed forms of colonial power and are thus doomed to failure; they are as useless and incongruous as the word *avenida* made to describe rows of pillaged and shuttered shops. The town—and, by extension, the entire colonial-cum-nationalist enterprise it represents—has two sources of possible redemption. One is to "go back to the desert," which, as the novel instructs us, is not a death wish but rather an opening up to the unpredictable but ultimately affirmational energies that permeate the desert landscape. The other source of hope resides in the "Arab fishermen in anonymous rags." Uncanny reminders of a much longer colonial history in the Maghreb, they also suggest the possibility of a lived, material futurity in their improvisatory repurposing of the "dilapidated movie house" where one can still almost imagine the dim flickering of Hollywood dream-images on a torn silver screen.

In other words, we are presented with a vision of cross-cultural communication and understanding very much at odds with what we find in other fictional texts that deal with ill-fated encounters between East and West in the colonial Maghreb, texts such as Bowles's *The Sheltering Sky* (1949) and *Let It Come Down* (1952) or Albert Camus's *Exile and the Kingdom* (1957). My aim is not to scapegoat Camus or Bowles on behalf of a set of recuperated Beat writers, but with such writers—Gysin, to be sure, but also Kerouac, Ginsberg, and even Burroughs—determined to see precisely the "connection" that remains mostly foreclosed in Camus' and Bowles' work, we have a very different conception of one's relation to the Other and to the world at large. For example, Camus' response, wider philosophical commitments notwithstanding, to the "Algerian question" remained strongly colored by his *pied-noir* background. In "The Guest," the best known of the six stories published as *Exile and the Kingdom*, the interactions between the French Daru and the unnamed Arab prisoner are characterized by an almost utter inability to communicate. Their isolation from one another— undoubtedly meant to stand in for the larger colonial and native populations in French Algeria—is reinforced by the desert landscape in which Daru and the Arab find themselves. Unlike the Sahara in Gysin's novel, in "The Guest," the desert lies under an "unchanging" sky that "shed[s] its dry light on the solitary expanse where *nothing had any connection with man* [*rien ne rappelait l'homme*]" (93, emphasis added).

In Camus' story we have a situation much closer to what Burroughs derides as "this inscrutable oriental shit" in reference to Paul Bowles' fiction (qtd. in Edwards 158). Brian Edwards has written eloquently about the various ways in which Bowles alternately evades and falls prey to the "orientalist trap" in *The Sheltering Sky*, and it is Bowles' second novel (the first to be set in Morocco), however, that bears most immediately on the present discussion. Bowles and Gysin were travelling through North Africa together while Bowles was composing what would become *Let It Come Down*, and from the beginning Gysin took a strong, almost proprietary interest in Bowles' work in progress. He lobbied hard for Bowles to change the name, and in late 1951, Bowles even wrote to publisher John Lehmann, asking, "Do you prefer Fresh Meat and Roses to Let It Come Down as a title? Brion Gysin has been insisting for so many months that a change should be made that I no longer have so strong a faith in my judgment" (*In Touch* 230). (Bowles would end up using Gysin's suggestion as the title of his novel's pivotal third section.) *The Process* is in many ways a rewriting of *Let It Come Down*, one that seeks to resolve its intractable questions concerning cross-cultural engagement and interaction. For one thing, Gysin's Hamid closely resembles, in his manner and narrative function, Thami Beidaoui, the keef smoking guide and companion of Bowles' protagonist, Nelson Dyar. Gysin's novel exists entirely within the imaginative space opened up by the climactic scene in *Let It Come Down* in which Dyar witnesses a bloody Sufi ritual and feels, for the first time in the novel—maybe his entire life—a sense of participation and oneness with the world around him. In Bowles' novel, however,

Dyar's ecstasy is only fleeting, and precipitates a descent into madness and murder by the novel's end.[8]

This entire discussion of Gysin's novel began in cinematic terms with a camera tilting down on Hanson's desert caravan. Hamid later describes the traumas of "the Whale" as being "like a movie," and a movie house features in the above passage depicting the ruined postcolonial capital. It seems appropriate, then, to close this essay with the suggestion that the novel's images of colonialism in ruins anticipate the more surreal moments of a film like Coppola's *Apocalypse Now* (screenplay begun in 1969), especially the scene, restored to the 2001 *Redux* version, in which Willard and his crew chance upon a French plantation—a spectral imperialism implied by this final outpost of western civilization. In *The Process*, the surreal, hallucinatory temporalities of "keef time"—full of gaps and distortions but also unexpected juxtapositions and sudden revelations—represent not an evasion of "present time," not a disavowal of the past's demands on us in the present, but rather their more profound apprehension in accordance with a worlded sense of history's multiplicity and non-linearity, of the past's immanence within the present moment.

Finally, *The Process* primes readers to reevaluate a whole range of Beat texts. Especially at this crucial moment in Beat Studies when charting the transnational dimensions of the Beat movement has become a clear imperative, Gysin's novel helps us reassess the tangled web of interests and interactions that binds Beat writers to the wider world. A central conviction of this essay has been that *worlding* is an anti-orientalism, and as a thoroughly worlded text in all the ways I have attempted to describe, *The Process* moves us far beyond standard appeals to the sublime sameness of Kerouac's "worldwide fellaheen" (following Spengler's *Decline of the West*) that have obscured for too long the complexity of Beat engagements with emerging world and post-colonial spaces. Worlded writing, and worlded critical procedures, will necessarily be attentive to cultural and historical specificity; they will have "refused," as Christopher Connery puts it, "to let only the West serve as a vantage point on the world" (*Worlding* 7). Gysin's novel and others, including *The Yage Letters* and *Naked Lunch*, the writings collected in Gary Snyder's *Earth House Hold*, di Prima's *Revolutionary Letters*, Amiri Baraka's major essays "Cuba Libre" and "The Revolutionary Theatre," and Ted Joans' poetry are similarly relentless in their attempts to link particular places, in the fullness of their spatial and temporal singularity, into much larger networks of struggle, liberation, and insight that remain firmly rooted in local, lived experience.

Notes

[1] Because the cut-ups seem to be a natural extension of Burroughs' formal breakthroughs in *Naked Lunch*, they are often credited to Burroughs alone, but he would insist on calling it "the cut-up method of Brion Gysin." The fullest and most authoritative account of the Beats' Paris years remains that of Barry Miles in *The Beat Hotel: Ginsberg, Burroughs, and Corso in Paris, 1957-1963* (New York: Grove, 2000). For Miles's discussion of Gysin, see in particular ch. 6, 8 and 9. Gysin provides his own characteristically transmuted account of 9 rue Gît-le-Coeur in *The Last Museum*, a novel that he had worked on since the late 1960s but ended up being the final work he published before his death in 1986.

[2] Gysin's article, with an accompanying demonstration of his and Burroughs's method, first appeared in *Evergreen Review and was published later that year in Brion Gysin Let the Mice In.*

[3] See Edwards's excellent work on Burroughs and Bowles in *Morocco Bound: Disorienting America's Maghreb, from Casablanca to the Marrakech Express* (Durham, NC: Duke UP), especially ch. 4 and 6.

[4] At the other extreme of what Edwards calls "the orientalist trap" is this desire for a too-easy identification with the Other. The best-known example of this phenomenon in Beat literature has to be Sal's claim in *On the Road*: "They thought I was a Mexican, of course, and in a way I am," uttered after a single day picking cotton with Terry and her migrant family.

[5] Gysin took Rolling Stones guitarist Brian Jones to Jajouka in 1968 and later provided the liner notes for Jones' *Pipes of Pan* recording, and jazz pioneer Ornette Coleman would also visit and perform with the Master Musicians.

[6] While in the Canadian military, Gysin met the great-grandson of Reverend Josiah Henson, who had been the model for Harriet Beecher Stowe's "Uncle Tom." Gysin was inspired to write *To Master—A Long Goodnight* (1946) as an update to Stowe's novel (Geiger 64-65). It was Gysin's long coda on "The History of Slavery in Canada" that earned him a Fulbright in 1949.

[7] Given Lévi-Strauss's appearance in the text, plus the fact that Mya's organization calls itself "GRAMMA," a "splinter-group of something called 'Logosophy'" (207) and the novel's highly performative critique of logocentrism in general—Hanson's final mission is *"to rub out the Word"*—it becomes very tempting to posit at least some knowledge of deconstructionist philosopher Jacques Derrida on Gysin's part. Although Derrida's *Of Grammatology* was first published in 1967, just two years before Gysin's novel, these tantalizing allusions probably extend no farther than the more immediate referents of the Himmers and Scientology.

[8] Hanson, of course, attempts to sustain Dyar's experience of inclusion and understanding by any means necessary. The contrast between Bowles' and Gysin's

novels neatly corresponds to the very different relations to Morocco and Moroccan culture that each writer had cultivated. At one end of the spectrum is Bowles, who, after four decades in Tangier, remained unambiguously western in his dress and demeanor and highly critical of the "Rousseauesque" fantasy of "going native" (*Conversations* 77). At the other end is Gysin, who often wore a traditional *djellaba* and was considered by Bowles to have "gone native with a vengeance" (qtd. in Geiger 92). Each represents an opposing aspect of the "orientalist trap." In the former, cultural difference tends either to be reified or insurmountable; in the latter, such difference is all too easily overcome.

Works Cited

Bowles, Paul. *Conversations with Paul Bowles*. Ed. Gena Dagel Caponi. Jackson: UP of Mississippi, 1993. Print.

---. *In Touch: The Letters of Paul Bowles*. Ed. Jeffrey Miller. New York: Farrar, Straus and Giroux, 1994. Print.

Burroughs, William S., and Allen Ginsberg. *Yage Letters Redux*. Ed. Oliver Harris. San Francisco: City Lights, 2006. Print.

Camus, Albert. *Exile and the Kingdom*. Trans. Justin O'Brien. New York: Vintage, 1986. Print.

Geiger, John. *Nothing Is True, Everything Is Permitted: The Life of Brion Gysin*. New York: Disinformation, 2005. Print.

Gysin, Brion. *Back in No Time: The Brion Gysin Reader*. Ed. Jason Weiss. Middletown, CT: Wesleyan UP, 2001. Print.

---. *The Process*. Woodstock, NY: Overlook, 2005. Print.

---. and Terry Wilson. *Here to Go: Plant R-101*. San Francisco: Re/Search, 1982. Print.

Wilson, Rob, and Christopher L. Connery, eds. *The Worlding Project: Doing Cultural Studies in the Era of Globalization*. Santa Cruz, CA: New Pacific, 2007. Print.

"Hard Blows of Love (Pick up on it like a horn, man, & blow)": Stuart Perkoff's "Round About Midnite" and Community Formation in Venice West

William Mohr

Donald Allen, editor of *The New American Poetry* (1960), the most influential anthology of poetry published in the United States since World War II, alluded in a brief introduction to the enthusiastic association between that volume's contributors and other "avant-garde" outlets such as abstract expressionist painting and jazz.[1] While *The New American Poetry* (*NAP*) notoriously organized its cartography of contributors in such a way that the rhizomatic links between its diverse communities ended up needlessly blurred, the writers associated with the Beat insurgency still managed to jostle their poetics with a hybrid interest in other art forms. Very little of the poetry published in *NAP*, however, revealed actual, direct links between jazz music, its musicians, composers and critics, and communities of Beat poets, even though their affinity for jazz music, both as a signifier and as an active collaborative force in public performance, was widespread public knowledge.[2] With few exceptions, the intermingling of jazz and poetry has generated only superficial commentary in public sphere media and obligatory, brief nods by academics in the past half-century.[3] This paucity of scholarship is partially the result of a focus on all but the most famous figures and communities in Beat writing, thereby privileging a literary excavation that exhibits only a single layer of the complicated relationship between jazz and poetry. If, as Louis Montrose has observed about another period, "All representations of power are appropriations of power," then questions about the appropriation of jazz by Beat poets and communities deserve to have a more substantial theoretical context than merely embedding this poetics in a cold war milieu. For instance, how might recent theoretical considerations of the ethical aspects of poetry's connection to the social contract ascertain the status of poets who perceive themselves as relatively *powerless*, even as they verbally generate images intended to alter the dystopic premises of the military-industrial complex? Then again, are representations of powerlessness equally capable of deconstructing power's efficacious logic? This essay will examine the 1957 verse jazz play "Round About Midnite" ("RAM") by Stuart Perkoff (1930-1974), the leading poet of Venice West in Southern California, and will consider how that play might increase our understanding of how theatrical dialogue, composed as a poem, enabled a community of Beat and/or anarchistic poets to interrogate the public performance of jazz music as a means of making its domestic, sonic poetics visible to its immediate community.[4] First, though, we need to review some of the biographical evidence that establishes the pertinence of Venice West and its poets to any larger project of literary movements tethered to community by the ligatures of aspiration and the fault-lines of social abjection. Specifically, how does Perkoff's long documentary-style poem, "The Venice Poems," written concurrently with "RAM" in 1957 and 1958, portend the role of jazz music within that community's earliest struggles to combine cultural activity with its need to secure sustenance and a minimal livelihood?

As I pointed out in a chapter on Venice West in my recent book, *Holdouts: The Los Angeles Poetry Renaissance 1948-1992* (2011), two founding members of Venice West, Stuart Perkoff (1930-1974) and Bruce Boyd (1928-1969, disappeared), had poems in *NAP* that either epitomized editor Donald Allen's claim about the poetic DNA of the avant-garde or served as a direct comment on the differences between various poetic communities on the West Coast. Both Perkoff and Boyd were far from provincially isolated poets. Perkoff had spent several years of his youth in New York City in the late 1940s and knew the founders of the Living Theater as well as anarchist poet Jackson Mac Low. Bruce Boyd had grown up in San Francisco; in addition to being an early friend of Gary Snyder's, he was also a close friend of Jack Spicer, through whose mentorship he became an active member of the Berkeley Renaissance. Both Bruce Boyd and Stuart Perkoff were subsequently eliminated from Allen's follow-up anthology, *The Postmoderns*, which most probably contributed to the diminished status of Venice West as a major site of Beat insurgency. Sarah Schrank's recent study, *Art and the City: Civic Imagination and Cultural Authority in Los Angeles* (2009), reiterates the critical consensus that Venice West was the "runt sibling of ... New York's Greenwich Village and San Francisco's North Beach." This characterization primarily developed because of the detrimental impact that Lawrence Lipton (1898-1975) had on the public's perception of Venice West in the late 1950s. Schrank describes Lipton as Venice West's "most famous resident," but that was only true when Lipton was alive to remind people of the success of his book, *The Holy Barbarians* (1959). Lipton's best seller, however, which had exploited "lesser-known" figures of Venice West, such as Stuart Perkoff and Charles (Charley) Newman, by turning them into emblematic caricatures for his so-called cultural jeremiad, has lost whatever freshness with might have once seduced the gullible. Instead, a poet such as Stuart Perkoff is finally establishing an adamant claim for canonical positioning; in particular, the publication in 1997 of Perkoff's *Voices of the Lady: Collected Poems* has provided a working volume for scholars to draw upon in order to assess the complexity of Venice West as a community important enough for Allen to have taken note of in his introduction to *NAP*. A volume such as *Voices of the Lady* enables us to understand the actual accomplishment of a truly representative Venice West poet such as Perkoff rather than be distracted by the author of a minor best-seller.

In examining Venice West as a quintessential Beat community, one discovers that the chronotope of its urban milieu had an extraordinary impact on its development. In the decade and a half after World War II, Lawrence Lipton description's of Venice as "a slum by the sea" was only a slight exaggeration.[5] Venice, however, stood in much more substantial contrast to the automobile-oriented city of Los Angeles than similar communities in New York and San Francisco did to their larger environs. This contrast shows up, in particular, in Stuart Perkoff's "The Venice Poems," a thirty-five page combination of lyric meditation and excerpts and adaptations of letters and journal writing that addresses the city of Venice in a manner reminiscent of Charles Olson's *The Maximus Poems*.[6] Like Olson, Perkoff was fond of walking both day and night in his environs, an ambulatory city within a nascent freeway city:

> debris & clots of dead moss
> scum the surfaces of the canals of venice west
> ....
> across a wooden bridge into a moon-hip world at nite
> the silence shattered by the deep rituals of cricket & dog
> the fish wings gently splat the water stillness with plopping sounds
> the great white dancer/moon
> up thru the shadow of the wood bridge
> life behind the housefronts/ imminent/ pressing
> .....
> step by step, up the ocean front walk
> towards the brite noise at the pier
> past houses & hotels, for old
> people
> ......
> it is peaceful to walk, there, at nite
> under the limitless black bloodlustre eye
> to feel life pressing/pressing from the houses
> to hear fish, dog, cricket, sing
> to walk high & leveling into the exploded mirrors of sunrise
> (Voices 256-258)

In this poem, Perkoff is attempting to generate an intersection of the baroque origins of the city, as evidenced in its architect Abbott Kinney's mildly demented duplication of an Italian city-state, and his own personal wanderings. "History," argues Michel de Certeau, "begins at ground level, with footsteps." Many of Perkoff's poems reflect his insistence on the importance of a scale of human perception that is much slower than twentieth-century modernity would seem to encourage. Even as he demands a simplification of urban scale, Perkoff simultaneously wants his perception of the poem itself to reassemble with the fluid, juanty acuteness of "exploded mirrors." For Perkoff, the metaphor would be the quality of the unit that each step constitutes in de Certeau's argument about urban life:

> [Each step] cannot be counted because each unit is qualitative in nature:a style of tactile apprehension and kinesic appropriation.... The motions of walking are spatial creations. They link sites one to the other. Pedestrian motor functions thus create one of the "true systems whose existence actually makes the city," but which "have no physical receivability." They cannot be localized: they spatialize.... Walking affirms, suspects, guesses, transgresses, respects, etc., the trajectories it "speaks." All modalities play a part in it, changing from step to step and redistributed in proportions, successions, intensities that vary with the moment, the route, the stroller. The indefinable diversity of these operations of utterance. They cannot be reduced to any graphic tracing. (105 – 108)

In splitting up urban pedestrian motion so that it resembles a variant of Zeno's paradox in which movement never achieves resolution and therefore spins off into inarticulate apprehension and connotation, de Certeau suggests that a furtive individuality can allow people to escape the grasp of modern planning. Perkoff's poem, on the other hand, makes it clear that even if this level of evasion of authority and control was possible in earlier stages of primitive surveillance, those who chose to resist in this fashion often subjected themselves to the tribulations of mental instability. Almost exactly at the same time as Allen Ginsberg was writing and then giving the first public reading of his prose poem "Howl," with its famous opening, "I saw the best minds of my generation destroyed by madness," the poets in the nascent community of Venice West were enduring an unusually high degree of psychological travail. Perkoff refers to this inaugural crisis in his community in a very long, single-spaced letter to Donald Allen written in two installments (dated March 12 and April 6-7, 1958):

> [F]ive people have gone insane in my living room. I say that as no joke. I mean, have gone over the edge, taken that journey, to the land where the metaphors are real, "as hard as/stone," yes actual, & poems, & pain, man, much pain, is shared out on the community, the materials from which the community & the traveler had to forge his or her rite of passage. To bring them over safely.

> So far, most of us have made
> it, but all the blood of all the travelers flows now in the veins of all. Pain,
> shared, caused, received, sacrifices, teaching – man, & that's just the
> beginning. A tightness, there between the people.
>
> (Donald Allen Archive, Box 10, Folder 26)

If Venice West as a community of disaffiliated poets eventually disintegrated, the
surprise is that it lasted as long as it did. The amount of anguish that individuals
in this community endured is extreme, even by the eccentrically oscillating
standards of avant-garde bohemia. One never hears any nostalgic yearning by
contemporary Southern California poets for the glory days of Venice West. So
many of the poets and writers ended up in prison or enduring neglect as poets.
Charley Newman, for example, who in one of his poems gave the name "Venice
West" to the community, is mainly remembered now through Perkoff's poems and
journal entries:[7]

> my friend is insane.
> wild with words & love
> he flows constantly.
> …
> charley newman has sad eyes.
> he looks into his sad eyes
> & sees a mixer of cement
> grinding & crushing
> its horrible noises grabbing
> at the child's brain
> while he sleeps.
>
> he riffs in the voice
> of a hurt child
> & he sees things.
>
> the concrete mixer that makes the obscene noises
> he pours himself into
> trapped with the rest of us
> in the dead street car.
>
> blood filling his armpits & his mouth
> he does not despair

but strikes at the hinges & padlocks
with hard blows of love.

("Portrait," *Voices of the Lady: Collected Poems* 164)

Perkoff's description of one of Newman's childhood nightmares provides a vivid specificity to the harrowing resistance that individuals tried to mount in the late 1950s. The asphyxiating power of the dysfunctional family structure displays itself as a concrete mixer, and those who operate the concrete mixer are merciless: if their orders are to fill a broken street car with people trapped inside, the cement flows. One of the prisoners refuses to be submerged, although resistance does mean that he will have to find himself united ("pours himself into") with the very thing he resists. Despite the sensation that he is being overwhelmed, the prisoner of this nightmare refuses to surrender. But is the mixer so amenably prone to reductive symbolism: is it simply a figure of personal repression? Or is Newman's vision, as recorded by Perkoff, an extension of the political despair being experienced by "ex-radicals"? Political opposition seemed futile, and it was much more than a question of confronting the predatory aspects of capitalism. The travesty of Stalin's rule had finally been acknowledged, and the movement of Soviet tanks into Hungary in 1956 did little to resurrect any hope that communism meant anything more than another aggressively bureaucratic military state.

Although most of the poets associated with Venice West eventually developed an archaic poetics in which the feminine was conflated with the stereotypical configurations of the Muse, Perkoff's "Venice Poems" are distinct from the Kerouac-Ginsberg-Burroughs group of Beats in that Perkoff includes women as individuals who are also being driven insane in the attempt to create an alternative community. Perkoff's poem does echo Olson's *Maximus Poems* in many ways, but none of Olson's letters present a scene as harrowing as the one that Perkoff reports in a long letter he embeds in "The Venice Poems." Perkoff appears to have saved a copy of a letter he wrote on July 9, 1956, to someone named David.[8] I do not know whether the letter was first written in verse or if it was typed as prose and then revised as Perkoff worked on the poem over the course of its year-long composition (July 2, 1957 – July 2, 1958):

there were too many things for her to see
she cd not sort them out

 into herself & me, the world & time
  into space & history
    she sent her eyes & vision

the warps & stones & enveloping structures
    she saw thru
        or around

until she came to that point in her mind
    where they were of enormous size
        & shapes completely without reference

& she sd: "hit me, feed me, rape me, touch me
    do something real to me, that I may know, touch, have
        something real to hold to. I
        must have something to
        hold to."

there is only so much that can be accomplished
by love.
beginnings are growing things.
there came a boundary, & I against it
stunned all my sharpness.

                          (*Voices* 261)

Perkoff's account in "The Venice Poems" of his wife's breakdown, which did lead to Suzan Perkoff spending two months at Camarillo State Hospital, adds different details to the event than are found in Lawrence Lipton's *The Holy Barbarians*, where Suzan is described as taking off some of her clothes in Lipton's living room. In both cases, Suzan Perkoff does not speak for herself.[9] If she was allowed to be part of the journey with the men, she still does not seem to have managed to write about the event so that her version was also recorded. In retrospect, we know that it would not be long before the voices of women began to be heard. Sylvia Plath's *The Bell Jar* (1963 U.K.; 1971 U.S.) and Anne Sexton's *To Bedlam and Part Way Back* (1960) would reveal the kind of mental anguish reflected in the statements by Suzan Perkoff that were quoted by her husband. Stuart Perkoff includes himself in the debasement of madness near the end of the letter to David in "The Venice Poems":

        there came that boundary
  & I, exhausted
        had nothing more to give

& only saw insanity in her eyes
& in my own.

(*Voices* 261)

If the formation of the community in Venice West encountered incommensurate boundaries of sanity and debilitating psychological implosion, the poets also saw themselves as being able to cross other boundaries. Perkoff and his other companions, including painter Saul White (1932-2003), were direct participants in the public performance of poetry and jazz, a partially improvised form of music in which the performers were expected to take risks that would encourage its listeners to break through the rational control of musical composition and reunify the divisions of body and soul imposed on social consciousness by Western philosophy. Jazz music provided a safety valve for the tortuous reassembling of the communal poetics of Venice West as a marginal community. Perkoff's theatrical conjoining of jazz and poetry enables the incommensurately expository logics of verbal art and the incremental logic of music to merge in a collage that empowers both expressions of imaginative expression.[10] The goal for the poets in particular is for them as an audience to disown passivity and reclaim its always already potential to play a role in the construction of poethical power.

"Round About Midnite"
Venice West and the Jazz-Poetry Movement

When Donald Allen asserted that contemporary poetry deserved to rank with jazz music and abstract expressionist painting as America's contribution to the avant-garde, he should have mentioned that at least four of the poets (Lawrence Ferlinghetti, Jack Kerouac, Philip Lamantia, and Stuart Perkoff) in the anthology had already decided that there was no reason to keep different art forms separated in their public presentations. If collage was the dominant artistic strategy of the 20th century, then one distinctive cultural collage was the attempt of poets and jazz musicians to collaborate. Rexroth and Ferlinghetti were among the first after World War II to take the stage with jazz musicians, attracting the attention of jazz critic Ralph J. Gleason in May 1957. Six months later, Gleason's verdict on the experiment was blunt and caustic:

> Mostly the poets are slumming. Jazz already has an audience and they don't. They're cashing in on the jazz audience but they won't learn anything from jazz or listen to it or try to allow the natural jazz rhythms they have to come out. Instead they are blithely wailing away with the same sort of thing that lost them their audience in the first place.... Not until a poet

comes along who learns what jazz is all about and then writes poetry will
there by any merger. What we have now is a freak, like a two-headed calf.
(*Downbeat*, 11/14/57; cited in *Holy Barbarians* 217-218)[11]

In citing this review in *The Holy Barbarians*, Lawrence Lipton claimed that his
"own experience disproves many of these allegations." In coming to Rexroth's
defense, Lipton was simultaneously positioning himself so that his leadership
of a young set of Beat poets and writers in his own neighborhood of Venice
West would achieve an homologous status with Rexroth's master-of-ceremonies
renown in San Francisco. Both Rexroth and Lipton shared many biographical
features: both were born in Chicago and were autodidacts; both struggled to
make a living as free lance writers engaged in a variety of creative and critical
projects. In recounting his role as performer and organizer of the West Coast Jazz
and Poetry Festival in the Crenshaw district of Los Angeles in December 1957,
Lipton claimed that jazz composer Benny Carter and trombonist Jack Hampton
approached him about putting on a show that combined poetry and jazz and that he
had already experimented for more than a year with poets reading their work with
music. While suspicion might be justified that Lipton was making this assertion so
that he would not merely appear to be imitating Rexroth, it does appear to be the
case, although the testimony given by Stuart Perkoff, the witness who can verify
Lipton's account, ends up damning both Rexroth and Lipton. In the previously
mentioned long letter to Donald Allen, Perkoff reported in extensive detail his
horrendous experience of working with Lipton on the concert. According to
Perkoff, Lipton did not consult any of the poets of Venice West or musicians that
he had worked with in experimenting with jazz and poetry before deciding to
invite his old friend Rexroth down to Los Angeles from San Francisco to headline
the festival. This invitation outraged more than the poets; according to Perkoff,
jazz drummer Shelly Manne (1920-1984) telephoned Lipton and rebuked him:
"by god rexroth was not going to come down here & give poetry & jazz its first
sounding in la after all the work we've put into it. . . ." Manne, in fact, was not
invited to be part of the festival, but his reproach of Lipton as well as Lipton's own
statement imply that jazz musicians and poets had been sounding out each other in
private rehearsals for a substantial amount of time, perhaps as early as the summer
of 1956. Certainly, Perkoff was deliberately writing poems for what he termed the
"jazz/poetry scene" as early as January 1957, as recorded in his journals:

It seems to me I am exploring new areas of language & idiom lately.
There is in my recent verse, I think a new religiousness, extensions of the
use of hip jargon beyond what I had ever thought possible, evidence of a
firmer control, of rhythm & of form. Like I think I'm building to a real

scene, something wild & erotic.

    (as it's the love that will love that refuses my poems lately that swings them so)

    something for the jazz / poetry scene --

    I wonder if it wd be possible to do "For S.W. of the wild nites" but it says cunt! A word not usually heard on jazz records -- probably not. too bad. But this "Alba" I hope will be suitable. (dated 20.I.57)[12]

              (Perkoff Archive, UCLA, Box 1, Folder 4, yellow cover)

However long Perkoff, Lipton, and musicians such as Manne had been experimenting together, the process required that Lipton overcome serious skepticism from both poets and musicians. The poets, according to Perkoff's letter to Allen, "laughed. didn't really think it wd work (especially as we knew Larry was no jazz hound." Perkoff claimed, in fact, that Lipton did not even own any jazz records until he met the poets of Venice West, "only some folk records and blues." Manne, on the other hand, said he had no interest in working with poets and would only consider combining writing and music if a musician read. Eventually Manne changed his mind, and Perkoff and White read their poems with Manne's band to each group's mutual satisfaction.

    Lipton was almost 60 years old, more than twice the age of Stuart Perkoff, who regarded Lipton as "very square" politically, even if the two had met through a socialist friend they had in common. Lipton apparently allowed his seniority to make assumptions about the privileges of rank, for he seriously miscalculated the willingness of younger artists to render service to his vision as unpaid initiates. If the patina of community is created by making promises and keeping them, Lipton began to scour the surface before the first sheen had faded. Perkoff and his friends, including painter Saul White and poet Bruce Boyd, and their wives and girlfriends were supposed to do all the work:

              we, the venice poets & their women ...wd: distribute the posters, thousands of them, do all the mailing, typing, deliverys, designing, publicity, contact the dj's, & c

        everything.

for nothing. no bread. no attitude of cooperation.

        so it turned out that saul & I had to force our way onto the stage to read our own poems.

           saul's poem almost didn't get done at all.

        (1 to 5)

bruce's verse wasn't being done, no.
charley newman's, no.

  4 poems by lipton.
                patchen.
                                Kenneth devoted ten or fifteen minutes
each nite to a ghastly rendition of a boring translation of a bad poem by
francis carco which he seems to think swings very much.
   ....
               so. I was supposed to get paid for reading. got fucked. got
lied to, man, it was terrible. all of us. we were supposed to have our
paintings hanging in the lobby, tony scibella was to choose. two days
before the opening he tells us/
                                             nada.
                                             nyet.
         (Perkoff's letter to D. Allen, Perkoff Archive, UCLA,
         Box 1, Folder 4, yellow cover)

Perkoff at this point had a wife and two young sons, and he was in no position to work for free. The discrepancy between the work done to make the festival a success and the division of the proceeds may have influenced Perkoff's evaluation of Rexroth's performance.[13] The "ritual drama" that Perkoff saw as the best possibility for jazz and poetry as a collage of art forms required more talent than Rexroth was capable of bringing to the stage:

               he doesn't make it with the music. his verse doesn't have
the rhythms, & neither does he. he can't even keep time. & this bugs the
musicians, man, something terrible. they dig to blow with people who can
keep time.
               & kenneth is up there shucking the people, giving them a
lot of bullshit in his kansas baptist preacher tone, which he seems to think
is prophetic.
         (Perkoff's letter to D. Allen, Perkoff Archive, UCLA,
         Box 1, Folder 4, yellow cover)

The musicians who were "bugged" were among the best known in West Coast jazz: Short Rogers, Bill Holman, Ralph Pena, Buddy Collette, Red Mitchell, and Marty Paich. Lipton claimed that it "took three nights and six performances" for the show to achieve any flow between the poets and musicians because only one of two scheduled rehearsals took place. If Perkoff, White, Boyd, and Newman had been allowed to take full turns on the stage instead of Rexroth and Lipton, however, the evening might have received better reviews.[14]

Perkoff's disenchantment with Lipton's conventional approach to a melding of jazz and poetry in a concert format did not dissuade him from pondering other means of configuring some kind of collaboration. Rather than read his own poetry to jazz music, Perkoff hit upon the oblique dramatic device of writing a "play" in which every character would speak in verse in the presence of jazz musicians, whose response would serve not so much as intermingled commentary, but as a face-to-face effusion of spontaneous community. Perkoff's five-scene verse play *Round About Midnite* had several performances in Venice in the summer of 1960. To call it a play, though, without qualifying that description would be a major error, even though Perkoff does mention in his journals a verse play he wrote in 1952 called "Metamorphosis by the Sea," and one can find an untitled short dramatic monologue by an anonymous struggling novelist, accompanied by fairly substantial stage directions, in his journals of 1961. The published script of *Round About Midnite*, however, in *Voices of the Lady* lacks all but one brief stage direction. Subtitled "a poem for voices & music," there is only one indication of where the music should come in, but no hints of how long it should last. In other words, this play has a libretto with an almost infinite catalogue of music awaiting new renditions.[15] The "voices" are of characters who are named "poet," "hipsters," "dealer," and "chick." Slightly over 400 lines long, "RAM" requires a cast of at least five people and would probably be best staged with at least seven people available to play the roles. A jazz ensemble is also obviously required, size to be determined by the stage director and producer. The hipsters have a significant plurality of the lines, with the poet and the dealer sharing an average of 115 lines each. Not surprisingly, perhaps, given the well-known patriarchal proclivity of most male Beat writers, the role of the "chick," who does not appear until the second half of the play, is consigned a very small portion of lines, although her lines do contribute significantly to the culminating thematic revelation.[16]

In dramatizing the problematic relationship of a verbal art being conflated with musical performance, Perkoff choose to make the poet a provisional protagonist. In bringing together the well-known challenge of social life in which individuality must somehow reconcile itself with the needs of the group, Perkoff's musically propelled poem seems to reiterate the observation that John Lowney made about jazz music being the exemplary demonstration of a truly democratic experience. Each musician, Lowney points out, gets to solo ("each sound has its own voice") and yet must do so in a way that the "one voice" is still intact. Perhaps Perkoff's homage to the jazz standard "Round About Midnight," though, should be considered more as a pedagogical poem than a drama in that the character known as "poet" is instructed about the importance of accepting one's role in the ensemble. The training that the poet must undergo emphasizes the need to wait and to submit to the results of an almost unfathomable patience. The characters of the hipsters and the dealer take the lead in reminding the poet of the arduous acceptance his role in the performance requires:

> *hipsters*
> you come on so strong, man
> pushing pushing
>> don't blow too hard
>> the reed splits
>
> the sound gets harsh & ugly
> no man can blow with you
>
>> in those rooms
>> where you've been hassling the word
>
> sit & dig
> sit & dig
>>>>> ("RAM," *Voices* 235-236)

The poet fears that he will never be able to overcome his internal conflicts, "the screams, man / the splinters & fragments." When the poet claims that "it never stops / the screams, the fragments," the dealer intervenes and reassures him that "there will be time / in yr broken cell / when the ice will melt / & the beat begin to pound." Nevertheless, the dealer cautions the poet that he must be prepared for the possibility that his essential contribution may be far different from what he aspires to make.

> *dealer*
>
> but if the cat who wrote the book
> has it in for you
> & you never get to solo
> & you have to sit up there & make that drone drone
> & never get to blow
>
> then dig that drone, man
> that's yr sound

> & dig that silence, man
> that's yr sound

("RAM," Voices 237)

On one level of poetics, silence functions as the ontological state that the poet is striving for in his relationship to the musicians. His words are not meant to call attention to themselves, but in their very restraint are part of the ritualistic preparation for the acceptance of the "space between the grooves" as the most significant dialogue between the poet and the musician and the audience.

When asked about "the sound" he is trying to achieve, the character called "poet" replies:

> *poet*
> like I listen
> & hear what I can
> & if there's no sound
> then that's [sic] the sound
> > *hipsters*
> even in the spaces
> between the grooves
>
> > *poet*
> then that's [sic] the sound

(Voices 239)

However, the poet is not the most important role in the play and to organize the performance around the poet would result in distorting Perkoff's primary concern in the play, which is to articulate an alternative social contract between the individual and a community that defines itself as outside of the normative expectations of America's "Disneyfication," a term that Lipton appears to have been the first to use.

In reading "RAM," one might think that the musicians are silent; in point of fact in terms of the "script," the musicians are indeed limited to their instruments. Textually speaking, though, the musicians should literally receive some authorial credit or attribution in any program notes that might accompany future productions of "RAM." Significant portions of the third part of "RAM" appears to be a redistribution of the lines "spoken" by Shelley Manne in an "Untitled" poem that is relegated to the "unpublished poems of the 1950s" section of *Voices of the Lady.* That this "Untitled" poem represents an actual transcription of Manne's hyperflailing collage of urban and human self-awareness would stretch credulity.

For all we know, Manne may well have been on a roller-coaster monologue in which he kept circling back to certain thematic timpani and Perkoff managed to notate enough on the spot and sufficiently recollect the rest to catch some of the sonic outburst, which he then made use of in "RAM" without any reference to Manne being the speaker. On the other hand, Perkoff may well be completely inventing this monologue or using only hints of what Manne said in order to create a jazz "character," which he then altered in a redistribution of lines to other characters in "RAM." In order to facilitate the presentation of this overlap, I will interject the names of the characters throughout the "Untitled" text as a means of showing the interplay of the "solo" version and the distribution of the lines among the "ensemble"'s characters. Perkoff introduces the poem's dictation with an indented overture:

> Shelley Manne, (sic) wild & out of his mind
> with the need to sound, the music & his rhythms,
> with not a waste beat or tone, each rap & stroke
> so sharp & clean as to blind the ear, on the
> night of August 13, 1956, sd/

> [*hipsters*]
> the city streets
> of hard
> Iike sharp things
> punching the eyes as they are
> walked
>   & black
> with dirt & blood

> [*dealer*]
> seeming the
> death of all human rhythms
> horns & thorns
> blasting all eyes eyes
> until there are no earth spots
> for feet to grasp
> to communicate

> [*hiptsers*]
>   They have their rhythms
>   They have their drums

They have their song

[*dealer & hipsters*]
throbbing the head
with blood filled eyes

expanding ecstasy wombed
in the soul

until it threatens to
explode the boned skull

[*poet*]
they have their magic
& their Gods

somehow breaking thru
the crusted earth

somehow once again
filling the air with fresh

[*dealer*]
somehow once again
 singing swinging singing

Perkoff's incorporation of the "Untitled" poetic monologue by Manne into "RAM" stops eight lines short of its finish as a separate piece "performed" only by the reader's imagined intonation of Manne's voice. In a tripartite assignment of Manne's speech to the hipsters, the poet and the dealer in their roles in "RAM," Perkoff is extrapolating the poetics of a jazz musician to dramatize how the community hears itself as a potentially replicable ("somehow once again") invention of social time and space. It is the recitation of Manne's speech by all of these characters that provides a way for the community to delimit its self-reflexivity through the influx of music. By refusing to accept its identity as a prosthetic terminal of a peculiar genre, such as poetry, perhaps this textual interweaving may be the major point of interaction that enables a community of poets at the margins to establish its own subversive, recuperative legitimacy.

Nor does Perkoff stop there: he collages his own writing, so to speak, in the remainder of the third portion of "RAM"; a dozen pages later in *Voices of the Lady*, one can find two consecutive short poems, parts of which immediately follow the redistributed lines from the "Untitled" poem in which Manne speaks. Both of these poems attribute either subjective perceptions ("wild & wail / the inner voice") or frenetic exclamatory declarations to Thelonius Monk ("Eyes! / is! / the! / thing!"). The latter is spoken by the dealer a total of three times in the play, spread out over two different scenes. Furthermore, Perkoff also inserts a portion of another part of "The Venice Poems," a section entitled "Voices Heard In Venice," in which Monk is quoted as saying "eyes, / man! Eyes. Mark the chalk of life / on yr eyes" (section 1, Part VI, "The Venice Poems" 278). Perkoff verges on suggesting that the performance of the text will achieve an efficacy through the willingness of the performers to take on the roles of an audience for whom the stage is the site of reified plasticity. In placing these imagined figures of the dealer, the hipsters, the poet, and the chick alongside the musicians, Perkoff breaks down the passivity that marks an audience as audience and makes the entire composition—verbal and musical – one voice:

> chick
> then the fire that I tend
> eats away the rotted structures
> burns pure & holy thru the eye
>
> dealer
> in the swing group
> each sound has its own voice
>
> hipsters
> yet all have the one voice

It should be noted that both "RAM" and "The Venice Poems" conclude with the same invocation of love as the elusive ideal and the source of a community's agency. Although this paper cannot accommodate the kind of theoretical argument about the ethical program suggested by Emmanuel Levinas and examined in a book such as John Wrighton's recent volume, it is worth noting that the emphasis on face-to-face engagement as a primary precondition for ethical action finds another correlation in Perkoff's "The Venice Poems," in which the final lines read:

> the place
>   has many
> real faces

> yes, there is a kind of
> knowing, it can be called
> love.
>
> ("The Venice Poems," *Voices* 289)

By the time "RAM" was performed in Venice in 1960, Perkoff was already in the early years of his heroin addiction.[17] The presence of the dealer in "RAM" was not merely an homage to the ubiquitous consumption of heroin within the world of jazz musicians, but an invocation of outlaw agency whose presence confirms that a poet or artist has assigned himself to a perfidious exile. Perkoff subsequently left Venice and spent time in Mexico, where hard drugs were easier to obtain and much less expensive. After an automobile accident in which fellow Beat poet Bill Margolis was seriously injured, Perkoff returned to Southern California and Venice. The following entry from his journals of late August 1964 depicts a poet whose addictions have rendered him asunder:

> The canals are still a place of repose. A refuge of still water & children's voices. Each house different from neighbor -- each so thoroughly *lived in* -- the people conscious, I am sure, of their uniqueness of habitat -- I have always wanted to live over here. Maybe someday I will. It feels so safe over here. I don't mean just from the police -- the people do not feel aggressive to me.
>
> I hope it is time for me to shed the role of permanently displaced person. It is statelessness carried to the extreme degree of peacelessness. For a long time I have had no rest. I want it to end. . . . I pray the lady needs me more settled now. The pen in the hand is the best feeling. How I stay loaded. . . . No protection is offered the wanderer. "It's a well-known fact that you're a brave man, Perkoff." Don once said to me. The streets! The streets!
>
> Still, they draw me to them. I will be out there tonight, most likely. Long since have ceased to ask "why?" Never get an answer to that one.
>
> Venice is filled with my past. An old collage stuck on the wall?
>
> (Perkoff Archives; emphasis added)

After Perkoff was arrested on drug charges in 1966, several people in the community made efforts to assist him legally or to provide comfort in his incarceration. Lipton recorded a long conversation with Venice West poet Eileen Ireland (born 1930) about different ways of helping Perkoff. Ireland mentions the possibility of a poetry reading to raise funds, but counters that suggestion by reminding Lipton that the last time such a reading was staged to help Perkoff, he himself was the major draw and obviously that was not going to be the case in the present moment. In the course of the conversation, Lipton mentions that Perkoff has been the subject of a French television show. No legal counsel could possibly save Perkoff, however; he had long overplayed his hand as a drug addict and was incarcerated for three years in prisons at Chino and Terminal Island, near San Pedro. He was not paroled until 1970, after which he lived for two years in Northern California. His sojourn up the coast enabled him to reestablish himself as a working poet. Among other writings, he composed a book-length poem, *Alphabet*, over the course of a year (April 8, 1972 – April 8, 1973; Larkspur, California), in which he made use of his understanding of the Jewish alphabet as a referential horizon line. For the first time since his original appearance in *New American Poetry*, his poems began appearing in anthologies. He settled in Venice once again in 1973, but within a year was dying of cancer. He gave his last poetry reading at Papa Bach Bookstore in West Los Angeles to a full house, but he was too weak to read more than a few minutes. Shortly after his death, Beyond Baroque magazine ran a picture of him at the reading as the cover of its magazine.[18]

In looking at Stuart Perkoff's published writing as work that deserves a sustained inquiry as a substantial contribution to Beat literature in the three decades after World War II, one is struck by how often the figurative language of jazz interweaves itself with Perkoff's addresses to the immediate members of his community. Such configurations are meant to be contextualized within Perkoff's definition of a city as "a place to / blow, to die, a / limit & / a tool" ("The Venice Poems," *Voices* 255). If the city is a tool designed to release communal energy, then the point of that release is to give a voice to the solitary individual so that the music of the community can respond with solace. An "Untitled" poem, for instance, in which Perkoff records one man advising another in the course of an argument, begins: "Take that everything's wrong, now, / & no one knows why," and concludes with a passionate imperative:

> pick up on it like a horn, man, & blow
> it'll swing you along
> inside you it lays naked and evil
> it's waiting to be born
>   get hip, Man, get with it
> before
> it gets with you.
>   (*Voices* 194)

In citing this advice to "blow," the communal development that awaits the transformation of that which "lays naked and evil" is love. At this point, let us return to the poem that Perkoff wrote for Charley Newman, one of the three people to whom "RAM" is dedicated. In summoning possible means of resistance, that poem concludes with the line "the hard blows of love." If love, in its ability to embrace the wounded and disfigured, is to have its functionality within the discourse of a social contract brought into full amplitude, then Perkoff proposes that the "hard blows of love" are not simply that which must be endured with renitent generosity, but that which issues forth as an encompassing utterance of a tangible continuity. If the initially held breath of skeptical disbelief can be released from its pent-up nihilism, Perkoff seems to suggest, then exaltation will breathe and blow like a horn.

In the final passage I have quoted, I detect the potential for a more complicated argument than I have sketched out for the present purposes, which largely were concerned with providing other scholars with the rudimentary knowledge of Venice West as a site in which jazz music met its kindred spirits in a turbulent public sphere of political recriminations and juridical attack. Is there an ethics underlying this antiphonal social dialogue? Is the counterpoint of yearning and aspiration by the "poet" in "Round About Midnite" the face-to-face acknowledgement that must be enacted and staged for our post-existential address and redress to have any ultimate social indemnification? Whether scholars are prepared to admit the full complement of Beat scenes, such as Venice West, to the discussion about "poethical trajectory" remains at the rear of the stage, like instruments yet to be attuned to each other.

Notes

[1] In the preface to *The New American Poetry*, Donald Allen specifically valorized the poets he selected as an avant-garde, who all shared "one common characteristic: a total rejection of all those qualities typical of academic verse." The doubled emphasis on the absolute in Allen's proposition ("*total* rejection of *all* those qualities") suggests that a rigorous program of alternative poetics had been at work during the decade and a half surveyed by his anthology, yet a close, comprehensive reading of public statements, letters, and journal entries of the poets chosen by Allen as representative of the next increment of the avant-garde would most certainly reveal more than a few instances of lingering affinities with traditional forms, themes, and prosodic affection. One example is the final portion of Jack Spicer's poem "Imaginary Elegies," in which Spicer handles iambic pentameter in four dozen consecutive lines as well as any academic in *New Poets in England and America* would ever demand. Even in Venice West, one of the most vigorous Beat communities to put into daily practice Donald Allen's imagined, antithetical prosodic utopia, classical forms remained present and accounted for. Eileen Ireland,

for instance, recalls that writing a sonnet was one of Stuart Perkoff's first writing assignments in his community-based poetry workshop in 1960, the year that *NAP* was published. Nevertheless, Stuart Perkoff not only shared with other better known Beat progenitors, such as Allen Ginsberg, Gregory Corso, and Gary Snyder, an exemplary commitment to whole-hearted, spontaneous recording of sensory detail, but also engaged in a far more diverse range of experiments. In particular, Perkoff's "Feasts of Death, Feasts of Love" could make a legitimate claim to be one of the most radical poems in all of *NAP* in terms of conjoining form and content.

[2] In *Life* magazine's article in which the Beats of Venice West were contrasted with the upstanding citizens of Hutchinson, Kansas, Lawrence Lipton was shown in a large photograph at the bottom of the first page reading his poetry to the accompaniment of a small jazz group (September 21, 1959; 31). Given this degree of mediated imagery in such wide-spread circulation, Allen's claim a year later hardly needed even token gestures of verification.

[3] Preston Whaley's "Blow Like a Horn: Beat Writing, Jazz, Style and Markets in the Transformation of U.S. Culture" (Harvard UP, 2004) is a recent study that distinguishes itself by considering the contribution of poet ruth weiss to the conflation of jazz and poetry in San Francisco in the late 1950s. Ginsberg and Kerouac, however, take their usual center stage position: "Jazz was the sound of *On the Road*" (197) and Ginsberg's "Howl" is riding shotgun. As might be anticipated, New York and San Francisco dominate Whaley's narrative. Venice West is cited so briefly one wonders if Whaley understands the scale of that community. Far more insightful and theoretically acute than Whaley, Maria Damon devotes an entire chapter to Bob Kaufman's poetry and its inextricable relationship to jazz in *The Dark End of the Street: Margins in American Vanguard Poetry*. Her project's primary topic is not jazz and poetry, however; figures involved in making recordings of jazz and poetry concerts, such as Kenneth Rexroth and Lawrence Ferlinghetti, do not make even a cameo appearance in her book. Richard Candida Smith's *Utopia and Dissent: Art, Poetry, and Politics in California* (1995) has a listing for "Jazz – influence on art and poetry" in its index followed by a citation of eight non-consecutive pages, none of which say anything of use about the topic. On the whole, though, the critical path thins out very quickly as we look further back. Michael Davidson's masterful study, *The San Francisco Renaissance: Poetics and Community at Mid-Century* (1989), notes that "certainly jazz exerted a powerful influence on the rhythms and phrasing of much Beat poetry," but the footnote contains only a single reference to a 1957 article in *Evergreen Review*. I would argue that Davidson's observation that "a bearded poet shouting poems to jazz in a dimly lit coffeehouse or raving on a street corner has become the popular image of what poetry amounted to during this period" (16) could be applied to academic writing, too, in its unwillingness between the mid-1950s and 1990 to

study in any extended formal way the cultural implications of the interaction of jazz musicians and poets.

[4] Towards the end of journal number 25 in Stuart Perkoff's archives at the Special Collections Library at The University of California—Los Angeles, Perkoff made a fairly substantial entry about "Round About Midnite," dated Tuesday, April 12 (1960), in which he observed that the play was set to be rehearsed that evening "at the VWC." The VWC is most probably a reference to the Venice West Poetry Center, which was located at 1108 Ocean Front Walk (*Coastlines* 8, 38). "The feeling is growing in me," wrote Perkoff, "of the importance of The Thing. Not the poem, I mean, although I think it is important.... This getting it onto a stage, where it belongs. Jesus Christ, it was written three years ago. & still the best use of hip language I know of although I somehow don't guess the production of it will make much difference to anyone or anything but me – maybe a few poets will pick up on what's happening & be turned on to some things about the sound -- ... [Le]Roi Jones said he'd like to see a collection of later work – I think I can put together one he'll dig -- & I asked Jonathan [Williams of Jargon Press] to publish 'The Venice Poems' – so perhaps we'll see."

[5] The residential evolution of Venice in the past half-century would easily serve as a case study for the process of urban gentrification, in which bohemian individuals and familial assemblages set up residence in the poorer quarters of a city, only to fall prey to real estate speculators who use the improved "tone" of a neighborhood in subsequent purchases and sales, thereby evicting those whose lives and work made the neighborhood more "habitable" from a middle-class point of view. If Venice was slow to become subject to this process, it was largely due to the vagaries of economic cycles in which development funds dried up in the mid-1970s and by the time relative prosperity returned, the California Coastal Commission made large-scale planning much more difficult. Although Venice ineluctably was gentrified, it proceeded at an incremental pace.

[6] Olson's influence on Perkoff can be noted in his journals, where he would quote lines of Olson's poetry. See box 1, folder 9 in Perkoff's UCLA archives in which he cites Olson's observation about human character being a process of revelation. Perkoff's correspondence with Olson in Olson's literary archives contain unpublished poems that did not appear in *Voices of the Lady*. "People don't change / They only stand / more revealed" is also quoted by Perkoff in his letter to David (Grossblatt) in part four of section one of "The Venice Poems."

[7] Charles Newman remains among the least known members of the Venice West community. I have not been able to ascertain either birth or death dates for him. A photograph of him about to start painting a canvas appears at the end of Lipton's *The Holy Barbarians*. Perkoff's journal (number 25) describes Newman's disappearance from the community at the very point at which "RAM" was about to be staged.

He appears to have been an illegitimate child and by 1960 had returned to living in a small apartment with his mother and sister. According to Perkoff's journal, Newman was the model for the role of the poet in "RAM." The play is subtitled "A poem for voices and music" and is dedicated to Charles Newman, Thelonius Monk, and Tony Scibella.

[8] The "David" to whom the letter in "The Venice Poems" about his wife is addressed might possibly be David Grossblatt (1920-1981), to whom a letter in the form of a poem is addressed in *Voices of the Lady.* A brief, but respectful obituary in *The New York Times* (June 26, 1981) described Grossblatt as a painter who "exhibited rarely," but who had studied with Hans Hoffman in New York City and in Paris after World War II. Perkoff's poem has the italicized subtitle *Concerning the disappearance of the "Two Musicians";* it would be a reasonable guess to assign Perkoff's letter to this painter, who was also the founder of one of NYC's first coffee houses, the Café Rienzi.

[9] For a more detailed account of Suzan Perkoff's mental struggles, see John Maynard's *Venice West: The Beat Generation in Southern California* (1991, 70-77 and 194-195). For further information about the marriage and children, see David B. Griffiths's *Beach and Temple: Outside Poets and Artists of Western America 1953-1995* (1998).

[10] In the concluding chapter of "Exiles from a Future Time," Alan Wald argues that "collage signifies a poetic reasoning unimpeded by discursive coherence" and claims that poets such as Muriel Rukeyser and Sol Funaroff made use of collage's "generative proximity" as a way to "articulate a vitality of spirit not rendered by any mode of representation given over to appearance (through the imagery of realism)" (320). Bringing jazz and poetry together would have extended the poetic reasoning of collage even further away from the bounds of discursive coherence and thereby challenged the grip of hierarchical authority on the spontaneous community taking root in Venice.

[11] Gleason's review would seem to constitute a reversal of his earlier willingness to lend his name to the album cover liner notes for an LP recorded off of a half-dozen performances of jazz and poetry by Ferlinghetti and Rexroth at the Cellar nightclub in San Francisco (Whaley 66-67). According to William Lawlor, both Philip Lamantia and Jack Kerouac gave poetry readings to the accompaniment of jazz music performed by David Amram in NYC in October 1957 (*Beat Culture: Lifestyles, Icons, Impact* 111). (Editors' note: the poet ruth weiss was also one of the earliest, if not the first, of the San Francisco poets, to perform poetry to jazz accompaniment.)

[12] Perkoff's estimate of his own ability to make resonant use of "hip jargon" was not self-flattery. In a foreword to *Voices of the Lady,* titled "For Stuart," Robert Creeley cites Bobbie Louise Hawkins's assertion that "Stuart Perkoff was the only

one she knew who could use the common street talk, the then-hip phrasing, in a way that felt undramatic, natural, not just an attempt to be like some other side of life or person." Creeley's foreword is dated June 7, 1997; Boulder, Colorado. "S.W." was Susan Weire (*Venice West*, 76-77). For journal entries about Weire dated 4.1.57 and 29.1.57, neither of which is quoted by Maynard, see the "yellow journal" (Box 1, folder 4). The former entry is at the bottom of a page with a poem entitled "Night Chasm."

[13] The address of the Los Angeles Jazz Concert Hall was 3020 Washington Boulevard. Rexroth's version of the jazz-poetry concert confirms Perkoff's implicit claim that the jazz-poetry concerts earned more than enough money to provide each of its performers a paycheck. In an interview with David Meltzer in the summer of 1969, Rexroth commented extensively on the relationship of poetry to jazz and recollected the sold-out four-night run: "Lipton staged the first big show. It was very successful, Shorty Rogers heading one group with me and Freddy Katz hearing the other. Lipton, Stu Perkoff, and some others. This was quite a show. And it ran for weeks and drew all kinds of people and made all kinds of bread" (*San Francisco Beat* 242). In this instance, Rexroth once again lived up to a reputation for exaggerating when he extends the run from four nights to "weeks," though he is no doubt correct about the financial success of the concert, which unfortunately only trickled down obliquely to Perkoff and his young family. In Rexroth's defense, it may well be that Lipton, as the concert promoter, paid him his promised fee and Rexroth assumed that everyone else got their cut of the proceeds.

[14] Maynard's *Venice West* makes only very brief use of an article and review of the four-night run (December 4-7) that appeared in the *Los Angeles Times* on December 3 and December 6, 1957. I call attention, therefore, to a short three-page article/review by poet Thomas McGrath that appeared in issue number nine of *Coastlines* (Winter 1957-58). The audience, McGrath noted, included Igor Stravinsky. McGrath cited Venice West member Saul White's poem as the "best received" of the evening because it "suggested or created an organic relationship between the poem and the music – something which occurred, to my way of thinking at least, only sporadically in the other readings. To some degree this happened in Stuart Perkoff's 'Alba' as well – this too was very well received – although there the voice dominated the music, and there was little of the interplay which this form requires. Worst relationship of words to music was in one of Lawrence Lipton's poems 'How Jazz Was Born.' .... Rexroth has an interesting thing with two basses, but his poem -- and Patchen's – cum piano is apt to remind one of certain disastrous Sunday afternoons spent in the parlors of people of (some) culture" (41). Perkoff's "Alba," by the way, is put into the section "Unpublished Poems of the 1970s"; this is not the only such instance in *Voices of the Lady*, and scholars should be cautious in using the book to match poems with any analytical chronology.

[15] Miles Davis's "Round About Midnight" was released in March 1957, which would correlate with Perkoff's journal entries about the dates of composition for "RAM." How much music from that album to use in a production of this play would be among a producer/director's first points of consideration, along with the question of how much of composer Thelonius Monk's original composition of the title song to present.

[16] The five scenes are each titled: 1. The Audition; 2. The Coming In; 3. Opening Riffs; 4. The Turning On; 5. Final Riffs: for full ensemble

[17] In *The Selected Poems and Prose of John Thomas*, the Venice West poet (1930-2002) recounts an occasion in late 1960 in which Perkoff stepped outside the Venice West Café and recited to him, without interruption, a long poem about the Warsaw Uprising, which Perkoff believed in his utterly stoned state to have been written down in his notebook. "Stu began to read," Thomas recollects. "I stood behind him – and since I'm tall and he was very short I could read the page as he read aloud. Reader, this was a great poem. A great poem. But… the poem he spoke wasn't the weak poem he had scrawled on the page. Oh, he would read a few words, maybe a line, from the notebook, then take off – pure inspiration – and blow stanza after stanza of magnificent poetry. It truly knocked me out. After twenty minutes he wasn't even looking at the page, but inward, at the poem flowing through him. Half an hour of this and he closed the book…." (109-110).

[18] Peter Levitt, a young poet who had studied with Creeley at SUNY Buffalo, arrived in Los Angeles shortly before Perkoff died. His poem in honor of Perkoff begins with a conversation with a clerk at the bookstore that was the site for Perkoff's final reading. The poem, "Books by Dead Men Make Me Hungry," was published in the fifth issue (Summer, 1975) of *Momentum* magazine.

Works Cited

Allen, Donald. Archive. Mandeville Special Collections Library, University of California, San Diego.

---, ed. *The New American Poetry*. New York: Grove Press. 1960

de Certeau, Michel. *The Certeau Reader*. Edited by Graham Ward. Oxford: Blackwell, 2000.

Golding, Alan. *From Outlaw to Classic: Canons in American Poetry*. Madison: The U of Wisconsin P, 1995.

Griffiths, David B. *Beach and Temple: Outsider Poets and Artists of Western America 1953-1995*. San Francisco and London: International Scholars Publications, 1998.

Lawlor, William. *Beat Culture: Lifestyles, Icons, and Impact.* Santa Barbara, CA:ABC-Clio, 2005.

Lipton, Lawrence. *The Holy Barbarians.* New York: Julian Messner, 1959.

Maynard, John Arthur. *Venice West: The Beat Generation in Southern California.* New Brunswick: Rutgers UP, 1991.

McGrath, Thomas. "Jazz, Poetry, etc." Eds. Mel Weisburd et al. *Coastlines,* issue 9, Winter,1957-1958, 39-41.

Meltzer, David, ed. *San Franciso Beat: Talking with the Poets.* San Francisco: City Lights, 2001.

Mohr, William. *Holdouts: The Los Angeles Poetry Renaissance 1948-1992.* Iowa City, IA: U of Iowa P, 2011.

Perkoff, Stuart. *Voices of the Lady: Collected Poems.* Ed. Gerald Perkoff, M.D. Orono, ME: National Poetry Foundation, 1998.

---. Archives. University Research Library, Special Collections. University of California, Los Angeles.

Russell, Charles. *Poets, Prophets, and Revolutionaries: The Literary Avant-Garde from Rimbaud through Postmodernism.* New York, Oxford: Oxford UP, 1985.

Schrank, Sarah. *Art and the City: Civic Imagination and Cultural Authority in Los Angeles.* Philadelphia: U of Pennsylvania P, 2009.

Smith, Richard Candida. *Utopia and Dissent: Art, Poetry, and Politics in California.* Berkeley: U of California P, 1995.

Sound recordings, Lawrence Lipton Papers, Collection no. 0159, Special Collections, USC Libraries, University of Southern California.

Thomas, John. *The Selected Poems and Prose of John Thomas,* Ed. Pegarty Long. Venice, CA: Raven Productions P, 2011.

Whaley, Jr., Preston. *Blows Like a Horn: Beat Writing, Jazz, Style, and Markets in the Transformation of U.S. Culture.* Cambridge: Harvard UP, 2004.

"Blow As Deep As You Want To Blow": Time, Textuality, and Jack Kerouac's Development of Spontaneous Prose

Tim Hunt

By and large, those of us who take Jack Kerouac seriously view him as an experimental writer, and this is so whether we locate his experimentalism in the April 1951 scroll of *On the Road* or in *Visions of Cody, Dr. Sax*, and other work that followed. Yet we have been only partly successful in coming to terms with the basis of his experimenting. As in that parable of the blind men describing an elephant, some of us have noted the ropey character of the tail, others the smoothness of the tusk, and so on. One feature that has yet to receive the attention it merits is Kerouac's sensitivity, even hypersensitivity, to the differences between speaking and writing as modes of language, how this put him at odds with his era's paradigms for fiction and textuality, and how this figures in his work, which can be read at least in part as an attempt to recast writing in the image of speaking and thereby reconfigure it as a medium. [1]

In his fiction Kerouac was not only resisting the ways a capitalistic society, based increasingly on consumption and conformity, threatened to erase the individual (matters clearly present in *On the Road*), but he was also responding to the impact of contemporary mass media – film, radio, recordings – not just as content but as new media in competition with writing. Kerouac sensed, I believe, not only how these media threatened print's hegemony as the dominant medium for creative work but also how they demanded new understandings of what writing itself is (or could be) and new writing practices – much as print's advent destroyed the hegemony of manuscript culture, altering writing as a medium and the nature of literature with it. For Kerouac, affirming "serious" literature as a "high art," while relegating "popular" literature and work in other media such as film to the banal limbo of "middle brow" or the sneering erasure of "low brow" was not an option. The impact of new textual media could not be evaded by privileging established norms of the literary (whatever the *Paris* and *Partisan Review* crowds might believe). Instead, it called for new understandings of writing as a medium and new understandings of literature. For literature to matter, new media had to be engaged, not simply ignored. And to engage Kerouac's work as it relates to these matters, one must push beyond *On the Road* to consider the experiments in writing, textuality, and fictional rhetoric that coalesced as *Visions of Cody*.

What the cultural anthropologist Jack Goody has termed the "literacy hypo-thesis" offers one way to begin to contextualize Kerouac's sensitivity to speaking and writing as distinct and potentially competing modes of language. [2]

Central to this position is the recognition that the development of writing converts speech, an aural phenomenon, into a visual system that can be stored outside an individual's biological memory, can be transmitted across space and time, and can thus be accessed through culturally mediated processes by readers. Writing makes it possible to give language a relatively stable material form and thus make it independent of the aural action of speaking/hearing, which cannot be stored, reproduced, or retransmitted (rather could not prior to the quite recent development of such technologies for analogue sound recording as the tape recorder). The literacy hypothesis underscores the multiple ways that writing's development has altered our cognitive relationship to language and how writing (and its subsequent extensions through print) has helped shape cultural forms and practices.[3]

For writers such as Kerouac who value oral practices, the usefulness of this perspective seems clear. Kerouac was compelled by the storytelling in the French Canadian neighborhood of his childhood, by "men talking in bars," and by the performances of such virtuoso performers of talking as W.C. Fields, Lord Buckley, and Neal Cassady, and he sought, clearly, a fictional mode that could express such voicings.[4] But he was also widely read (much more so than his image as King of the Beats suggests) and deeply committed to writing. How literacy might have had an impact on orality historically is, thus, necessarily secondary for understanding how a highly literate individual writing literature, such as Kerouac, might experience the dialectic of speaking and writing as complementary but far from identical modes of language.

As the title of Walter Ong's *Orality and Literacy: The Technologizing of the Word* suggests, the focus of literacy hypothesis has been largely on how introducing the technology of writing alters the oral as a medium and, as it were, overwrites it. Yet writers such as Kerouac necessarily function fully within the realm of literacy, whatever their sympathies for the oral practices.[5] Mid-century writers were neither pre-literate nor part of an oral culture being altered by the dynamics of literacy (whether one understands these dynamics as cognitive, institutional, or a combination of the two). In this study, then, the literacy hypothesis is a context for considering the interplay of speaking and writing in Kerouac's experimental writing but not directly its method, which derives more immediately from the linguist Josef Vachek, the media theorist Friedrich Kittler, and recent work in editorial theory, which in various ways examine writing itself as a medium.

Vachek's analyses of the oddities of spelling in English led him to conclude that alphabetic writing is a doubled system that can be used as a visual system operating without any necessary connection to sound (i.e., it can itself be language) or used to encode and store approximations of the sound of speech (in which case "writing" represents language but is not itself language). Writing, because of its doubled nature as a medium, can be used to enact quite distinct understandings of what language is, what writing is as a medium, and how writing and speaking relate to each other and to language. It is possible to treat the page as a space for enacting speech, which is then stored in writing with the reader reading as if hearing the poet speak. It also possible to treat the page as a surface on which one composes in writing much as a painter paints, casting the reader as a kind of viewer.[6] In *Gramophone, Film, Typewriter,* Kittler explores how both technological and institutional factors mediate the understandings writers and readers form of specific communications media. For Kittler, how writing functions as a medium at any point reflects both the nature of writing itself, how we produce and access it (writing in a manuscript culture and in a print culture are not identical systems), and differences in how writers and readers are acculturated into the medium (being taught that silent reading is preferred to voicing what one reads, for example). Similarly, recent work in textual studies and editorial theory has dramatically increased our understanding of how texts are initially generated in a field that includes not only the writer but also rhetorical conventions, economic institutions, and technological conventions, all of which become elements of the work and participate in its function and its meaning as it is generated, produced, circulated, and consumed.[7]

* * *

In one sense, Kerouac's decisive break with the paradigm of the modern novel – and his turn to rhetorical inventions discussed above – is the famed April 1951 scroll draft that, in revised form, became *On the Road* as Viking published it in 1957. In it, he begins recasting writing in the image of speaking and using writing as a medium for recording performance rather than a medium for composing. But our tendency to focus on *On the Road* has obscured the centrality of the writing Kerouac was doing later in 1951 and in the early months of 1952 – the work published posthumously as *Visions of Cody.* Yet it is in *Visions of Cody* that Kerouac first formulates the approach that becomes Spontaneous Prose, then explores ways to use it to achieve his goal of what he termed in a June 1948 journal entry as "'soulwork.'"[8]

Since its publication in January 1973, *Visions of Cody* has confronted readers with a basic question: is it a cohesive, albeit experimental, work or separate pieces – the literary equivalent to a sampler box of holiday chocolates. Reviewing the book for the *New York Times*, Aaron Latham argued for the latter:

> "Visions of Cody" is a bizarre book with a bizarre history. When Kerouac wrote "On the Road" in 20 days on a continuous roll of paper in 1951, friends like Allen Ginsberg read it and did not much like it. Kerouac had not yet invented the legend that he never rewrote anything, so he set to

work composing inserts, which he hoped would make his friends like his book better. These inserts, however, grew uncontrollably.... By the spring of 1952, the new sections were almost as long as the original.

At some point in early 1952, Kerouac decided not to use the inserts to patch up his earlier work but to consider them a new book in and of themselves. He called this new work "Visions of Cody." Kerouac was like a mechanic who had started out to repair a car with spare parts and had ended up building an entirely new vehicle instead. The form of the new book was no more what Jack Kerouac had set out to create than the form of "The Waste Land" was something T. S. Eliot had set out to create. It just happened, practically by accident, at least by indirection. "The Waste Land" achieved its disconnected quality when Ezra Pound cut out all of Eliot's connections; Kerouac's new book achieved its discontinuous structure when he decided to leave out the book for which his inserts had been written. He kept the repair parts but junked the car.[9]

He concludes that *Visions of Cody* should be read "in bits and pieces as if it were a book of poetry rather than a continuous narrative because it simply is not a continuous narrative."

Latham's view carries some weight. He had been researching Kerouac to write a biography and had at least some access to Kerouac's papers (then still held by the Kerouac estate and not then generally available), and he is right that *Visions of Cody* is largely, except for the final section that re-tells the events of Parts Two through Five of *On the Road*, without plot in the conventional sense. And Kerouac did generate at least one of *Cody's* sections as a possible "insertion," as he termed it, for *On the Road* as he looked to improve what he characterized (in a July 14, 1951, letter to John Clellon Holmes) as "spontaneous unartificed too-pure too-raw criticizable 'Road.'"[10] But the work journal he kept for the fall of 1951 shows that other *Visions of Cody* pieces were not drafted for *On the Road* but instead written as he searched for an approach to writing and fiction that would take him beyond the April 1951 scroll. Also, the initial handwritten drafts for some of the pieces in *Cody* show that he reworked them (in minor but telling ways) specifically to integrate them into the book. Moreover, the *Visions of Cody* typescript shows that Kerouac reordered at least some of the sections as he finalized the book, which suggests he was purposefully structuring the units.

While a few "bits" of *Visions of Cody* began as "repair" work for *On the Road*, Kerouac combined these "bits," the evidence shows, with units originally written for neither *Road* nor *Cody* and with others written specifically for *Visions of Cody* after he began thinking of it as a distinct project (the evidence also shows that *Visions of Cody*'s initial title was *On the Road* and that Kerouac initially expected it to replace, not supplement, the April 1951 scroll version).[11] Whatever its success or failure, *Visions of Cody* is a vehicle in its own right, not a box of "repair parts" to rummage in for a stray brake pad or a butterfly valve, and it is time to recognize that the book is more central to Kerouac's ambitions as a writer than Latham credited.

While *Visions of Cody* does (as Latham notes) derive from *On the Road*, it is not subordinate to it. In June 1948, as Kerouac was completing the primary draft of *The Town and the City*, he expressed his desire to help pioneer the novel of the future, which would "have all the virtues of Melville, Dostoevsky, Celine, Wolfe, Dickens and all the poets in it (and Twain)." His goal was, as he then put it, to write "A 'soulwork' instead of a 'novel,'" and he sensed that this would require developing a way of writing that would access and "preserv[e] the big rushing tremendousness in me and in all poets."[12] The April 1951 scroll draft of *On the Road* marks Kerouac's decisive break with the paradigm of "a 'novel.'" In it, he begins recasting writing in the image of speaking and using writing as a medium for recording performance rather than a medium for composing. In *Visions of Cody*, Kerouac formulates the approach that becomes Spontaneous Prose, then explores how to use it to achieve his goal of "soulwork."

Visions of Cody itself has to be the primary basis for evaluating Kerouac's recasting of writing in the year following the April 1951 scroll experiment, but two additional documents help clarify how he understood what he was attempting and why. The first is his July 14, 1951, letter to John Clellon Holmes, in which he shares his desire for a more radical approach to writing than he had attempted in the scroll *Road*. The other is the work journal covering August 28, 1951, through November 25, 1951, which includes entries that laid the conceptual groundwork for *Visions of Cody*'s experimental aesthetic. The mode of writing Kerouac developed in the scroll *On the Road* enabled the narrative momentum and direct address to the reader that he had been unable to manage in the more conventional attempts at *Road* that preceded it. In *Visions of Cody*, though, he first realized his dream of transferring at least some of the "rushing tremendousness" within him onto the page. In his prior work, Kerouac managed partial representations of "rushing tremendousness"; in *Visions of Cody*, he recasts writing's relationship to speaking and language and uses writing to perform "rushing tremendousness."

Kerouac's desire in June 1948 for his writing to be directly and fully his sense of "rushing tremendousness" anticipates his desire for what becomes, over the course of writing *Visions of Cody*, first sketching and then Spontaneous Prose. There have been a number of valuable discussions of Spontaneous Prose over the years that have addressed the charge that Kerouac's writing is artless, so neatly summed in the oft quoted Truman Capote quip that *On the Road* is typewriting rather than writing. These include John Tytell's chapter on Kerouac in *Naked Angels* (1976), Regina Weinreich's *Kerouac's Spontaneous Poetics* (1987), and Matt Theado's *Understanding Jack Kerouac* (2000). George Dardess' excellent 1975 essay, "The Logic of Spontaneity: A Reconsideration of Kerouac's Spontaneous Prose Method," is too often overlooked, perhaps because it is not a monograph, and Warren Tallman's 1959 essay, "Kerouac's Sound," remains a prescient, forceful account of Kerouac's style.

These discussions of Spontaneous Prose typically develop along some combination of the following three lines: (1) contextualizing Spontaneous Prose historically by linking Kerouac to such precursors as Wordsworth, Emerson, and Yeats; (2) attempting to elaborate Kerouac's provocative but idiosyncratic descriptions of how to perform Spontaneous Prose into a systematic aesthetic theory and orderly methodology; and (3) demonstrating that Kerouac's Spontaneous Prose writing is skillful and aesthetically rewarding. While valuable, these discussions do not address, at least directly, the possibility that Kerouac's search for a new mode of writing, for what becomes Spontaneous Prose, was driven in part by his sense of the differences between speaking and writing as modes of language. Spontaneous Prose is not, from this perspective, only a new writing practice. It is also an attempt to reconceptualize writing so that it can function as a medium for interactive behavior (as speaking does) and thus be a medium for performing rather than (in writing as conventionally understood and practice) a medium for composing.

Writing, as Walter Ong has argued, converts language from a medium operating in time to a spatial medium in which time is necessarily symbolic rather than actual (a point Kittler further develops). Spontaneous Prose is, among other things, an attempt to make writing operate in time and to prioritize the temporal over the spatial so that writing can be used not only to compose representations of speaking (what, in speech-act theory, would be termed "written utterance") but also to function as a mode of speaking (what might be thought of as "uttering" occurring in and as writing). In speaking, in actually "uttering," language is inherently behavioral; a speaker interacts directly with a listener.[13]

Spontaneous Prose is also an attempt to replace the conventional figure of the "reader" (who interacts with the writer indirectly through the mediation of the composed text) with a reading listener who actively participates in the writing as if with the figure of the writer. In Spontaneous Prose, the writer "speaks" in writing rather than "writes" in writing. Spontaneous Prose is, then, not only a specific practice of writing, it is a reconfiguring of what writing is as a medium, and through it Kerouac attempts to reconnect speaking and writing as expressive systems in spite of the way print literacy has deepened their inherent separation. Implicit in this is Kerouac's sense, I suggest, that writing and speaking are not simply different presentations of the same thing—language—one operating aurally and one operating visually with slight differences between the two because of this but that they are, instead, and to a significant degree, different things, different media. Discussions of Spontaneous Prose have typically emphasized Kerouac's procedure for writing rather than his reconceptualizing of writing as a mode of language and on its relationship to speaking and the dynamics of speaking. (For complementary discussions of Kerouac's orality and its bearing on Spontaneous Prose, please see John Hrebeniak's chapter "Orality: 'Mad to Talk'" in his study *Action Writing: Jack Kerouac's Wild Form* (2006), which focuses on the orally derived features of Kerouac's style and, especially, Nancy M. Grace's chapter "The Creation Story: Duluoz and Company" in her study *Jack Kerouac and the Literary Imagination* (2007). Grace's study is particularly valuable for its account of how Kerouac's desire for writing to be voiced, to be oral, is explicitly present even in his earliest apprentice writing and for connecting Kerouac's Spontaneous Prose to his spirituality as a way of demonstrating its centrality to understanding the Duluoz Legend.)

Kerouac's initial sense that the intense three-week effort of performing the scroll *On the Road* was a significant breakthrough is evident in his May 22, 1951, letter to Cassady, where he claims that he will use this new method for all his future projects and asserts that the "Book marks complete departure from *Town & City* and in fact from previous American Lit."[14] Two comments, though, suggest that he was still assessing the scroll. He admits, "I don't know how it will be received" and notes that he'd been working for "Thirty days" not simply "typing" the scroll onto sheets of paper (presumably so that he could submit it to Robert Giroux, the editor who had accepted *The Town and the City* and who was "waiting to see it") but also "revising" it (SL 317). Given his typing skills, Kerouac would not have needed "Thirty days" to type the scroll onto sheets of typing paper. And if the revisions had been simply breaking the scroll into paragraphs and replacing actual names with fictional ones, that would have added little time to the process. Kerouac was, it seems, working at improving the scroll as he typed, not just copying it.[15]

Whatever his sense of these revisions, by mid-July Kerouac was starting to see problems that he believed would need more than a paint job and polishing the chrome. His July 14 letter to Holmes (who had recently completed his first novel, *Go*) shows that one factor was that both his agent (Rae Everitt) and close friends (Ginsberg and Lucien Carr) were insisting that the book needed to be reworked to make it publishable. Another factor was Giroux's rejection of *On the Road* as Kerouac had typed it up from the scroll (SL 320). But Kerouac was also recognizing that *On the Road*, even if it "told all," was not yet the full realization of "Fiction" that he was after. He characterizes the scroll as "spontaneous unartificed too-pure too-raw criticizable 'Road'" and declares he is "ready to write '<u>Horn</u>' – immediately – another big 'creative' construction." The phrase "big 'creative' construction" apparently refers back to *The Town and the City* and probably as well to one or more of the abandoned attempts at *On the Road* that preceded drafting the scroll.

The dichotomy here between "too-raw" (which figures here as insufficiently transformed from the actual to the literary, as in not fully cooked, rather than too explicit) and "creative" defines the two impulses Kerouac had been trying to unite in his work, and he returns to this dichotomy later in the letter: "The On the Road that I've written now is the false one from the point of view of art – and yet it's the true one that happened." [16] This reflects his desire for a mode of writing – and a version of *On the Road* – that would be "true" to what "happened" (the "too-raw"), "true" to "art" (the "creative"), and "false" to neither. Another comment in the letter expresses this desire even more directly:

> —when I get to be so pure you won't be able to bear the thought of my death on a starry night (right now I've nothing to do with the stars, I've lied so far) it will be when I'll have come to know & tell the truth (all of it in every conceivable mask) & yet digress from that to my lyric-alto knowing of this land, this huge complicated inland sea they call America...

For Kerouac this would be "a 'deep form' bringing together of two ultimate & at-present-conflicting streaks in me." The dialectic of "truth" (in the sense of what "happened" in all its complexity and even contradictions) and "lyric-alto knowing" (subjective elaborations, even digressions, that would function as obligatos to the narrative in the way a jazz player responds to the vocalist's presentation of the melody) parallels what Kerouac terms, in the introductory note he wrote when New Directions published *Excerpts from Visions of Cody* in 1959, "just a horizontal account of travels" (implicitly the April 1951 *On the Road*) and "a vertical, metaphysical study":

> I wanted to put my hand to an enormous paean [*Visions of Cody*] which would unite my vision of America with words spilled out in the modern spontaneous method. Instead of just a horizontal account of travels on the road, I wanted a vertical, metaphysical study of Cody's character and its relationship to the general "America." [17]

This formulation suggests that Kerouac's dissatisfaction with the scroll *Road* in the letter to Holmes is that he had come to see it as just "horizontal" – an account that "telled all" but failed to develop the richness of implication (the "vertical" and "metaphysical"). His desire for a mode of writing that would simultaneously engage the "horizontal" and the "vertical, metaphysical" is what drove him, first, to attempt what Latham termed "repair parts," then to the more radical experiments that became *Visions of Cody*.

Kerouac's dilemma in July 1951 was two-fold. First, he had yet to find a way to write that would record the documentary "truth (all of it in every conceivable mask)" while also responding to "truth" in its various dimensions by following out the "creative" flights of "lyric-alto knowing." But to revert to the mode of *The Town and the City* or to the *On the Road* attempts that preceded the April 1951 scroll would be to revert to approaches that he had already found wanting. Second, making *On the Road* less "raw" and more "creative" would make it even harder to publish. In the letter to Holmes, Kerouac admits he "partially and maybe wholeheartedly agree[s]" with the "criticisms" of Ginsberg and the others of the *On the Road* typed up from the April 1951 scroll but then adds, "They want straight narrow easy roads." To indulge in the "lyric-alto" digressions would make *On the Road* a fuller record of his responses to what happened and a fuller record of the multiple dimensions of the truth but also make the book even less "straight" and "easy" – and less publishable.

Kerouac's letter to Holmes suggests that his initial strategy for addressing this dilemma focused on content and structure rather than trying to add "lyric-alto knowing" to the scroll.[18] He proposes deleting the scenes from Parts One and Two in which Sal travels by himself rather than with Dean (and saving them for a "future extensive novel"). He would, then, he explains to Holmes, complete *On the Road* with "insertions" that would "plumb Neal's depths" – a strategy that would have placed Dean clearly at the book's center and underscored Sal's role as observer and narrator by reducing his role as a character in the action.[19]

The usual view that Kerouac unreflectively typed up his experiences suggests that he lacked the ability to plan such structural changes much less consider their implications, but "[a]ll the reading" he reports he had been doing shows that he was not as naïve or ignorant as the usual view would have it. He lists Lawrence, Dickinson, Yeats, Whitman, Faulkner, Perse, Blake, and Flaubert (he praises "parts" of *Madame Bovary* as "excellent"). Perhaps most surprising, he also lists "Henry James' Ambassadors," which (not surprisingly) he finds "utterly worthless, without exaggeration," and notes that he had been reading "many prefaces." While he does not specify that the "prefaces" were James' prefaces gathered in *The Art of Fiction*, the placement of "many prefaces" in the list suggests that is the case. James' prefaces explore the interplay of point of view, tone, style, and structure, and Kerouac's probable awareness of James' analysis of these matters (plausibly another dimension of what Kerouac meant by "writ[ing] according to what they told me at Columbia University"[20]) suggests that he would have understood that his scenario for revising *On the Road* as presented in the letter to Holmes would have moved the book even closer to being a traditional realistic novel – a study of

Neal/Dean. This would probably have made the novel more acceptable to Giroux. But placing Neal/Dean fully and solely at the center of the novel, while simplifying the task of documenting the literal "truth" of the road, would have made it even more difficult to "digress from that to my lyric-alto knowing of [...] America."

In the letter to Holmes, Kerouac notes that he had already begun writing "insertions" for *On the Road*, but his admission that "the only real way" to "plumb" Cassady would involve "surrounding him with the perfect imaginary intense characters like the Imbecile, The Walking Saint & Pictorial Review Jackson" suggests that these insertions were more "horizontal" than "vertical," more "raw" than "creative," more "truth" in the documentary sense than "lyric-alto knowing." One reason for holding back from "plumb[ing]" Cassady through "perfect imaginary" figures, even though the letter shows this is what he wants to do, is that it would bring the speaker's subjectivity to the fore, which would conflict, to some degree, with the strategy of cutting the scenes from Parts One and Two. In any case, his sense that "This can be done later – a 'perfect' Neal" suggests he was already thinking ahead toward what would become *Visions of Cody* and that he was thinking of the "insertions" he was actually working on as a way to resolve the problem of how much *Road* was Sal's story and how much Dean's rather than a way to add "lyric-alto" digressions. Such cuts and "insertions," at least as Kerouac thought about them in July 1951, would have widened the shoulder of the road and filled some pot holes, but they would not have transformed *Road* from a novel of what "happened" into a "big 'creative' construction" with "lyric-alto knowing."

Perhaps most importantly, the July 14 letter shows that Kerouac, at least at this point, believed that the scroll *On the Road* had not achieved the simultaneity of "horizontal" and "vertical" that he was after, even as it shows that he had not yet fully diagnosed the problem or formulated a solution. While it is clear that he wanted to make *On the Road* more "creative" and less "raw," he also wanted to make it more publishable. But the recasting that would give fuller play to his renewed sense of "creative soul" would make the book less publishable. More-over, he wanted to move on to new work rather than deal with the dilemma of how and whether to revise the April 1951 *Road*. In the scroll he had hit on the strategy of talking through the narrator as a surrogate of himself and using the typewriter as a recording device to store this typetalking in writing rather than constructing a conventional narrator and composing written representations of speech for the narrator. But in the scroll *On the Road* he was still using a potentially radical approach to voice and writing to perform a relatively conventional novel – to present "just a horizontal account of travels on the road" (as he put it, implicitly referring to *On the Road*, in the introduction to *Excerpts from Visions of Cody*). In the conventional novel the full range and intimacy of the writer's own voice is not possible, in part because what would be said would be too digressive, too unconcerned with what Latham termed "continuous narrative." The mid-century norms for the novel – at least as Kerouac understood them in the summer of 1951 – could not accommodate "digress[ions]" of "lyric-alto knowing."

Implicit in Kerouac's July 14 letter to Holmes is a sense that the scroll *On the Road* hadn't gone far enough. But Giroux's rejection of the *On the Road* (as well as Ginsberg's, Everitt's, and Carr's criticisms) suggested he'd already gone too far, underscoring the risk of exploring how to achieve of "lyric-alto knowing." This is, I suggest, the initial context for what Kerouac was and was not doing with the "insertions" that Latham terms "repair parts." To the extent that he hoped to "repair" the car of *On the Road* to make it more publishable, he was actually looking to add material that would have made the novel more conventional, even though, as the July 14 letter shows, what he wanted to do was to commit to "lyric-alto knowing," which would make the novel less conventional and less publishable.

This conflict between fixing up *On the Road* for publication and exploring "lyric-alto knowing" threads through the fall 1951 work journal and leads to Kerouac's decision to put the April 1951 *Road* up on blocks and instead write what became *Visions of Cody*.[21] The first entry (written August 28 while he was in the VA hospital with phlebitis) shows, for instance, that he considered abandoning the scroll *Road* to make yet another attempt at *On the Road* as a relatively conventional novel, using the approach he'd used for *The Town and the City*:

> So I worked out second big "labor" of my writing-work-life: the Victor Duchamp On the Road epic, which I'll start as soon as I get home, using tried & proven system of Town & City—the "daily heap," belief, in fact reverence, humility, much solitude, walking, and now more health measures (less coffee, more tea; alcohol only before dinner, if any.) And a world-view backbone to the structure of the fiction. These Tolstoyan feelings…I welcome them back after almost 3 years floundering in "hipness" and dissolution and indecision and ambiguity.

The same entry shows that he had also been considering a potboiler, to have been titled *Hip*, as a way to make money to support himself while he worked on the projects that actually mattered to him, then realized he had neither the "heart" nor will to do so:

> To make a living, though, money for rent, food, money for future needs. First, in here I tried writing a potboiler; I said to myself "Like Faulkner I'll write a goodnatured watered-down monogram of my style, like Sanctuary, and make a living"; I'd call it "Hip"; but I don't have the heart for it. It may sound vain, but the act of writing seems holy to me, so much so I

can't even be a "hack" in secret; I can't put a beginning and an end onto something, which never started and never will end. Holy…sacred…to use the written word in honor of life, in defense of life against the forces of death and despair, to make old men lift their hearts a bit and women think (or cry), and young men pause before it's too late for <u>realizing</u> to do them any good—why use the word for cheap illiterate vulgar fools who buy books in the mass to titillate their empty beings between vices and hypocrisies.

Behind both comments is the problem of what to do with the scroll *On the Road*. In the August 30 entry he writes:

"On the Road" as I wrote it this last spring is still an existing work of 150,000 words that I ought to do something with — cut out, put in, sell. But again….that word OUGHT. I'm being consumed by an ecstatic sense of doubt; no greater joy than perfect doubt and all those masks.

Threaded with these strategies for resolving *On the Road* (or veering off to write *Dr. Sax*, which would have been almost entirely "creative" and "vertical" in the way he was then thinking about it and which he considers in several entries) are reflections that document Kerouac searching for an approach that would enable him to write without literary pretense (the "too-raw"), so that the writing would be "truth (all of it in every conceivable mask)," while yet including the "lyric-alto knowing" that would express his subjective responses to the multiple aspects of "truth."

The fall 1951 work journal shows that Kerouac saw himself as having three options. First, he could focus on writing as a way to make a living and revise the scroll *On the Road* for the marketplace. This might address his problem of how to support himself (even though *The Town and the City* had largely failed in this regard), but it would mean becoming – in actuality rather than ironically as he had put the matter in his October 6, 1950, letter to Cassady – a "redoubtable hack" and mean turning away from "us[ing] the written word in honor of life." A second option would be to commit fully to self-discovery and self-expression. This would allow him to focus on the interiority of "rushing tremendousness" and to "lyric-alto knowing" but would mean giving up on publishing with a major house like Harcourt Brace and leave him broke and dependent on his mother for a place to live and food to eat. Moreover, the entries suggest that writing as if only privately and for himself was finally too solipsistic for Kerouac; it was to invite the despair of Melville writing on in isolation to find an audience after the failure of *Moby-Dick*, and it was, as well, to turn away from the example of

Whitman and his hope to speak to and for the democratic you. The third option was to divide his time between writing for commercial publication and writing for self-discovery and self-expression. This offered a way to earn money yet remain committed to "soulwork." But it left Kerouac's two senses of what he was trying to achieve as a writer still in conflict and left the negative dimension of each in play and unresolved. The journal shows Kerouac alternating between exhorting himself to shape *On the Road* into a commercial novel (spinning out scenarios for doing so); wanting to renounce writing for commercial publication once and for all (considering scenarios that would make *On the Road* even less publishable than it was); and trying to convince himself to alternate between writing for publication and writing for self-discovery and self-expression. Most crucially, though, the fall 1951 journal entries offer glimpses of the experiments that led to *Visions of Cody* – experiments that relate more to working out how writing might become self-discovery and self-reflection than to enhancing *On the Road* for commercial publication. That *Visions of Cody* remained unpublished for more than twenty years after its completion shows that Kerouac had good reason to worry about the risk these experiments represented.

The discussions of writing in the fall 1951 journal focus on three overlapping matters: one is how to free writing more completely and decisively from the formal expectations associated with the figure of "the mysterious reader" in order to write as if engaging an actual other, the figure of "YOU," as he termed it in his October 6, 1950, letter to Cassady. Another is how to understand the differences between writing and speaking as modes of language in order to work out a way to write in which writing would function more as speech functions. And third is the question of how writing can become more fully a medium for performance rather than a medium for composing. *Visions of Cody* enacts Kerouac's responses to these questions, and as such it completes the reimagining of writing and fiction initiated, but only partly realized, in the April 1951 scroll version of *On the Road*.

Kerouac's development of what he initially termed "sketching," then later labeled Spontaneous Prose (when he summarized the approach in "Essentials of Spontaneous Prose") was one key in achieving *Visions of Cody*. In the October 16 journal entry, he writes, "'Make sketches, like painters,' says Ed White, and this afternoon I did, of old diner and old B Movie on Sutphin Blvd" (versions of these sketches appear in Part 1 of *Visions of Cody*, as do versions of the sketches he mentions in subsequent journal entries).[22] The importance of sketching is evident in the October 26 entry, where Kerouac notes that he has, that day, typed up some 1,800 words of his "main ms." (The October 18 entry indicates that this "main ms." was a version of *On the Road* that would have opened with the scene in *Visions of Cody* where Cody propositions Tom Watson to teach him pool followed by "the football-passing scene in the Denver dusk"[23].) He then adds,

but wrote much more than that and much better in my scribbled secret
notebooks that had better become my real work or I'm a failure – I am
not satisfied with those 1800 words – the notebook sketches are greatest
I've ever done...tonight I dashed off a sketch about the Bowery which is
completely without sentence form and is better than the greatest of my
sentences except the "heartbreaking loss" one but only because IT was
something special.

Kerouac's pleasure in sketching derives at least in part from the way it eliminated
the need to subordinate "lyric-alto knowing" to the narrative level in what he
here terms his "main ms." In sketching, the writer focuses fully and immediately
on what is being sketched, ignoring the "horizontal" dimension of narrative.
Perceiving the scene and responding imaginatively to it become a single
process. Writing is both the medium for recording this process and the means
of enacting this awareness, as the writer moves (as Kerouac put it in "Essentials
of Spontaneous Prose") from the "jewel-center" of the moment of interest out
through the associations the "jewel-center."

In sketching, the writer does not compose the scene; instead, the writer records
his attention to the scene at the moment of attention. As such, sketching creates
a record of the scene (converts it into a written object), but more importantly, it
records the process of the writer engaging the scene. Instead of the writing (the
result of the writing) becoming an object that transcends the time (and timing) of its
making so that the only dimension of "time" for the written object is the historical
time of its later production into printed commodity and subsequent circulation, the
writing that comprises the sketch preserves the elapsing of the time of its making;
the sketch continues to occur in and as the time of the process of its writing, because
it records the sequence of the writer noticing, engaging, and elaborating what is
being sketched. The sketch, even though it portrays a scene, functions less as a
representation (a composed object made of writing) and functions instead more as
a performance (the writing as the medium that records the process of attention).
Moreover, in the process of sketching the sketcher's initial subjectivity and the
inherent objectivity of what is sketched are not fixed points of perspective or stable
categories. The sketcher and scene are simultaneously present to each other, and
the sketcher both enacts the scene and is, in part, enacted in turn as he perceives
and projects the scene onto the page.

Kerouac's "old diner" sketch, which the October 16 journal entry indicates is
from his first day of sketching, illustrates the process. Written in pencil in a small
notebook it reads:

OLD DINER

There's nothing like the old
lunchcart that has the
old fashioned railroad car
ceiling and sliding doors—
the board where bread
is cut is worn down fine
as if with bread dust and
a plane; the icebox is
a huge Brownwood thing
with old fashioned pull-out
handles, windows, tile walls,
full of lovely pans of
eggs, butter pats, piles of
bacon—old lunchcarts
always have a dish of
sliced raw onions ready
to go on hamburgs—
Grill is ancient and dark
/ [   ] an odor which
is really succulent, like
you would expect from
the black hide of an
old ham or an old
pastrami beef—The
lunchcart has stools with
smooth slickwood tops—
There are wooden drawers
for where you find the
long loaves of sandwich
bread—The countermen:
either Greeks or have
big red drink noses [page break]
Coffee is served in white
porcelain mugs—sometimes
brown & cracked—An
old pot with a half-
inch of black fat sits
on the grill with a wire

fryer (also caked)
sitting in it, ready
for french fries
melted fat is kept
warm in an old small
    [white porcelain] [as if inserted after next line was written, then erased]
coffee pot,--A zinc
siding behind the grill
gleams from the brush
of rags over fat
stains—The cash
register has a wooden
drawer as old as the
wood of a roll top desk—
The newest things are
the steam cabinet, the
aluminum coffee urns,
the floor fans—But
the marble counter is
ancient, cracked, marked,
carved, & under it is
the old wood counter
of late 20's, early
30's, which had come
to look like the bottoms
of old courtroom benches
only with knifemarks
& scars & something suggesting decades of delicious
greasy food. Ah![24]

The sketch both presents an actual old diner and does not. The specific "Old Diner" becomes an occasion for the sketcher (Kerouac) to engage the resonance the scene has for him through the details. The diner is ordinary, yet oddly positioned in time and social space. The performance juxtaposes the old and worn with the new[er] ("aluminum coffee urns," etc.) and balances a delight in food that seems to have its roots in childhood memories with adult awareness of economics and class ("The countermen: either Greeks or have big red drink noses"). The sketcher's immersion in the scene (his subjectivity as opposed to his documentary awareness or objective distance from the details) is evident in the interplay of precise observation and metaphorical extension ("the board where bread is cut is worn down fine as if with bread dust"), and this immersion explains a modifier like "lovely" in "full of lovely pans of eggs, butter pats, piles of bacon." The modifier here does not add to the precision of what is being observed; rather, it registers the sketcher's reaction (Kerouac, that is, is not here aiming at Imagism and failing), and the interplay of tonalities are as much the action of the passage as the observing of details (as such, "lovely" has more to do with "sliced raw" than with "pans of eggs"). And the sense of emotional participation (the delight in food, the sense of being an outsider, the sense of things worn and discarded, including the people in the scene, and the sketcher's sense that he is both linked to and severed from them) builds to, and gives impact to, the sketch's final gesture – "something suggesting decades of delicious greasy food. Ah!" – which is, appropriately, an emotional action rather than a recognition or claim or climactic image.[25]

Sketching offered Kerouac a way to bring his emotional stake in his material – his "lyric-alto knowing" – to the fore. In sketching, the process of interacting with the scene being sketched as it is being sketched is what matters. Sketching is not telling a story; it is discovering one's response to the material in the present moment. As such, it is a tactic for using a physically present scene (and eventually, as Kerouac pushed his sketching experiments further, a remembered scene or imagined scene) to initiate the interiority of "rushing tremendousness," then using the conceit that one is simply sketching (without concern for "the mysterious reader" or a surrogate "YOU" and without concern for structuring a "novel" or even an extended work of "fiction") to allow "I," through the mediation of the "eye," to use the occasion of the scene to talk to (and onto) the notebook page as one sees, responds, and discovers the range of one's response to what is being sketched. In sketching, "lyric-alto knowing" becomes the same as "tell[ing] the truth (all of it in every conceivable mask)" rather than a "digress[ion]" from it, and this is at least partly the case because sketching, as Kerouac first conceived it, was a process that had no relationship to the goal of writing a book. For the sketching writer there is no "mysterious reader"; the sketcher is in dialogue with himself. As such, sketching is a self-reflexive performance, the "eye" of the "I" engaging the material to sketch and speaking it to the "ear" of the "I" as if the perceiving self is in dialogue with the responding and imagining self.

Kerouac's comments on sketching and the sketches from October and November 1951 make it clear that he never thought of them as "insertions" for the scroll *On the Road*, and the journal shows that he initially did not think sketching could be used to write fiction. Sketches were, as he put it in the October 26 entry, like a painter's informal "street sketches in pencil" done for his own satisfaction and separate from what he terms, in the entry, as his "main ms.," which he apparently sees as equivalent to the painter's "canvas oil job" done partly for art's sake but inevitably also to fulfill the expectations of others (whether that be the abstraction called the "market," a specific patron, or the preferences of a specific gallery). The question becomes, then, how Kerouac managed to reconceive sketching so that it could become a method for books such as *Visions of Cody*, not simply a private exercise.

The key is the centrality of process and performance in sketching. The eventual importance of sketching aka Spontaneous Prose did not derive from its informality as an activity, or entirely from its lack of concern with the audience so that the sketcher could focus on his own engagement with the material being sketched, or solely from the discovery that ordinary things could become the "jewel-center" for a spiral of observations and associations. These factors mattered, but what mattered more is that sketching is driven by the writer's engagement with the material at hand for the moment of sketching with writing functioning as a medium to record the performance. In composing a fictional system, in treating writing as a means to compose a written object in the conventional sense, the writer erases the actual stake in what is being written (the writer is the source of the fictional counters and the fictional structures but the art of composing is in part to screen this from the reader). In sketching, the sketcher's presence in the process is integral to the sketch because the sketch records the sketcher's evolving stake in the material. The sketch, that is, enacts the "seeing" of what is being sketched; it also enacts the engaging of what is being sketched ("greasy food. Ah!")

Kerouac's initial frustrations with the scroll *On the Road* – that it "telled all" but lacked "lyric-alto knowing" – and his uncertainty over how to proceed with it during the summer of 1951 and early fall suggest that he still regarded the scroll as something needing to be converted into a composed fictional system and that he had not yet recognized the possibility that performing writing could be a viable "method" for developing an extended work for readers rather than a brief piece for himself. The sketches of October and November of 1951 were one factor in Kerouac shifting to having the written performances themselves be the extended work of fiction. The fall 1951 journal documents two other factors – factors that Kerouac initially explored separately from sketching but came to blend with it as he conceptualized the "wild form" of *Visions of Cody*. What these factors and sketching share is that all three derive from Kerouac's growing recognition that the kind of writing he wanted to do needed not only to derive from performance but be performance and that writing should be a recording medium rather than a compositional medium.

Kerouac identifies one factor in the October 8 journal entry – "a great discovery of my life." The occasion was hearing the jazz alto saxophonist Lee Konitz, then early in his career, play at Birdland. Kerouac characterizes Konitz's "ideas" as "more white…more metaphysical" than the "Master" Charlie Parker. In Konitz,

Kerouac senses someone who is compositionally aware (as if "some Buxtehudian scholar of the dank gloomy cathedrals practicing and practicing endlessly in the bosom of the great formal school in which he is not only an apprentice but a startling innovator") yet also "in the first flush of his wild, undisciplined, crazily creative artistic youth." For Kerouac, the "discovery" occurs as Konitz plays "I'll Remember April" as he'd "never heard it <u>conceived</u> and as he [Konitz] never played again last night." For Kerouac, who believed he was "listening to a fellow who's doing exactly what I am…but an alto," Konitz,

> foresaw the tune straight through, took complete command of it, let measures of it carry it along of its own impetus while he busied himself <u>within it</u> with his own conception of it—a conception so profoundly interior that only the keenest ear could tell what he was doing, and this didn't mean David Diamond [the American composer who was a friend of Kerouac's and was apparently with him at Birdland that evening], it meant Cecil Payne [the baritone sax player who was playing with Konitz that evening and who, Kerouac notes, listens to the solo "in amazement"] (<u>and</u> me) (<u>and</u> others in the club)—beautiful, sad, long phrases, in fact long sentences that leave you hanging in wonder what's going on and suddenly he reveals the solution and when he does, with the same vast foresight that he brings to a tune you now understand it with vast <u>hindsight</u>—a hindsight you wouldn't have gotten without his foresight, and a hindsight that at last gives you the complete university education in the harmonic structure of 'I Remember April,' a beautiful and American structure to boot. And at a moment of his saddest, seemingly lost note which became found in the conclusion of the "sentence" I suddenly realized "He is doing exactly what I'm doing with a sentence like 'hints of heartbreaking loss that filtered in with chinks of October daylight from the street' and here I've been worried all along that people wouldn't understand this new work of mine because next to Daphne du Maurier it is almost completely unintelligible (for instance)!"—does <u>LEE KONITZ worry about VAUGHAN MONROE</u>? Let the dead and the dumb bury the dead and the dumb!

Significantly, Kerouac believes that Diamond, a noted composer, does not understand what Konitz is doing, while Payne, an improvising jazz musician, does. This suggests that Konitz's ability to improvise is what excites Kerouac. But what matters more is that Konitz, in playing this one tune, goes beyond the dichotomy of composing and improvising, precisely because he knows the song's structure and harmonic system (a "complete university education" in it) so well that he can use the "tune" not as something to express by playing it (performing the composition), nor as something to elaborate by generating variations from it (improvising from the composed elements), but as a means to engage and enact his own interiority. In the performance, as Kerouac perceives it, Konitz plays himself through the music rather than playing the music and thereby manages something more existentially real than the composition he draws on and something deeper than improvisatory elaboration. Moreover, through engaging his material with such great depth of knowledge and trust in his artistic power, Konitz is able to enact, not merely to comment on, "rushing interiority" so that some in the club "could tell what he was doing" and respond.

Kerouac finds in Konitz's "I'll Remember April" not only a validation of writing as process and performance but also an alternative to writing solipsistically for one's self (the danger in sketching as he first practiced it) or writing to meet the expectations of "the mysterious reader" (which threatens to reduce expression into product). The other option is to write for the few, like himself and Payne, who are able to hear and to not worry that people like Diamond (and Giroux) will fail to hear, in part because their formal, academic training makes it difficult for them to appreciate that what matters is not the materials of the art but how the artist engages the materials to enact "a conception so profoundly interior that only the keenest ear could tell":

> Do musicians and hip people and intelligent people run to hear Vaughan Monroe when they want to find out what's the latest development in American jazz or American music?—No, they run to hear Lee Konitz. Does Lee Konitz make a living playing these loomings of the monastic school for his peers and confreres? no, he makes his living some other way [...] Does Konitz try to tone down his imagination to make his music more understandable to the masses? He's not playing for the masses, he's playing for musicians and listening in the great up-going formal school, and he knows as much as Bach or Beethoven know, that the masses or at least masses of listeners would catch up and listen in the future and find their souls transformed, as his is, thereby: just as James Joyce knew that his Ulysses was but a prophetic image of styles of the soul to come, not a puzzle or any of that nonsense. Does Lee Konitz listen to the advice of well-meaning friends who say it's all in the heart [...] no Lee Konitz prefers to play alone, which is the same thing as with Tristano, that is interior music, the unspeakable visions of the individual (again) rather than tone down his mad vision in the name of heart or great or whatever shibboleths his well meaning friends have; or like John Holmes and Giroux telling me where my greatest power lies, whether they say "heart" or "simple" (dig that? a simple heart?) when all the time I have an unspeakable mad and beauteous

> vision for which I need mind more than heart (but not much more) to bring
> it out and nothing simple about it at all; like people in Ireland telling James
> Joyce to concentrate on Irish Naturalism, or in America telling Wolfe to
> concentrate on the really fine and worthwhile stories like you see in Good
> Housekeeping, or so on endlessly and now, talking about myself, the point
> disappears in any case my great decision I noted down in pencil in the
> gloom of Birdland at 2 a.m.—"Now—BLOW AS DEEP AS YOU WANT
> TO BLOW."

For Kerouac, Konitz in "I'll Remember April" transcends the dichotomy of
"cool" and "raw," studied and intuitive, composed and improvised and validates
performance as an artistic method. And he finds, as well, a way to reject the
advice of Holmes and Giroux that he simplify his fiction. Above all, he finds
the permission to perform his stake in his material as deeply as he can without
worrying about the conventional expectations of "the mysterious reader."

While Kerouac's comment in the October 13 work journal entry – "now what
am I going to do about that Lee Konitz business!" – underscores the importance of
hearing Konitz perform "I'll Remember April," it also shows that he was initially
unsure how to adapt his understanding of Konitz's approach. For one thing, blowing
"DEEP" in a nightclub for those able to hear is a different matter than writing
"DEEP" at one's desk as if performing for future (absent) readers one hopes will
eventually "hear" the writing, not merely read it. More crucially writing and
performing music are not directly equivalent. The more precise analogy for writing
would be writing music, not performing it. Both writing "writing" and writing music
involve notating in visual symbols, and these two procedures can each function in
two ways. Writing "writing" and notating music can each function as transcription
systems (visual encoding used to create approximate representations of actual
sounds); and they can each function as expressive systems in their own right, in
which the "writing" and the "music" that is produced is processed visually – i.e.,
by reading (highly literate musicians such as composers and conductors can read a
score and process the interplay of composed elements without having to hear them
played; this level of literacy is much more common among those who read writing).
Both writing "writing" and writing music not only enable the planful and recursive
construction that we term composing, they encourage it. The more direct parallel
to what Kerouac believes Konitz manages in his Birdland performance would be
between playing music and playing language, since both involve performing for and
to "YOU" – and such performing in language is usually more a matter of speaking,
of talking, than of writing. If Konitz's Birdland performance authorized Kerouac
to "BLOW AS DEEP AS YOU WANT TO BLOW," it did not offer a clear way to
rethink the nature of "writing" as a medium so that he could play in writing as an

improvisational musician would rather than use writing to compose as a composer (such as Diamond) would.

Kerouac's attempt to sort this out in the October 13 entry echoes his sense, in his June 18, 1948, journal entry, that he might be able to "preserv[e] the big rushing tremendousness in me and in all poets" by "spill[ing]" his "visions into a [wire-recorder] microphone" (WW 95). The entry opens,

> Jerry Newman said I would be great if I wrote like I talked [...] (not only Jerry but Carl Sandburg said "Sometimes you get literary, otherwise you're all right, just don't be literary, there's no need for it, don't worry about it, ha ha ha hee hee hee!" and he laughed and put his arm around me, real eccentrically (!)—s' fact.

The juxtaposition of to write "like I talked" and to not "be literary" suggests that Kerouac is here considering that writing as he "talked" might free him from writing in a self-consciously and reductively "literary" manner. This would also, a comment later in the entry suggests, involve shifting from writing as composing to writing as performance:

> It's recording and explaining the visions and memories that rush across my brain, in narrative or otherwise logically connected sections—such as dissertative—. . . what I had during a long happy walk. If I had a tape-recorder everything would be okay...just walk & talk.[26]

Kerouac would not fully resolve the implications of his desire to write as he talked until he wrote the "Imitation of the Tape" section of *Visions of Cody* sometime early in 1952 (discussed in the next chapter), but the October 13 entry shows him beginning to recognize that "talking" is a closer equivalent to what Konitz was doing musically than writing, and this seems to drive the desperation at the end of the entry, where he senses that committing himself to being a talker would mean turning away from writing fiction of the sort that an editor like Giroux might accept for publication:

> For the life and death of me I can't write ON THE ROAD...and I have to, I have to, or I'll just die off for God's sake. To hell with it—I'm going to write something else [....] but enough rules & childish talk. I am going to go on with what I started Sept. 16—God help me—the objective Dean Road— --

He's killing me—Good Christ and the trouble is there's nobody can help
me or give advice!—how much longer

No I won't do the objective Dean Road.

That the *On the Road* in this entry is the "objective Dean Road" suggests Kerouac
here is referring to his ongoing dilemma of what to do with the April 1951 scroll,
and if so, working to complete this *On the Road* would be to turn away from the
direction represented by Konitz's "I'll Remember April" and from the possibility
of writing as "I talked."

This dilemma over whether to complete *On the Road* as a relatively
conventional novel or to "BLOW AS DEEP" as he wanted was the immediate
context for Kerouac's first sketches. In the October 16 entry in which he announces
sketching, he adds, "Well by God I resumed writing today!" And while the obvious
analogy for sketching is visual art, not music, the simultaneity of the desire to
perform in language á la Konitz, to practice writing as a mode of talking, and to
sketch are, actually, three facets of a single impulse – to reconceptualize writing
and fiction in the image of speaking (with writing being a medium for recording
rather than a system for composing). And if this is so, the distinction Kerouac
makes between a painter's "street sketches in pencil" and "his canvas oil job" takes
on additional significance. The "canvas oil job" is not only a matter of working
to satisfy the market and its norms, it is also something that the painter produces
deliberately through construction. It is compositional; it is akin to writing in the
usual sense of the term. The "street sketches in pencil," however, are not only less
formal and generated quickly in the direct presence of what is being sketched, but
they are more akin to performance, more akin to talking. They are a process where
the sketcher talks to – and with – himself through the material that occasions the
sketch as he performs that material onto paper. And this is, also, to suggest that
for Kerouac sketching was equivalent to Konitz's "I'll Remember April" in the
way the external structure that occasions the sketch – in this case a scene rather
than a composed song – enables the sketching writer to perform both the scene and
his own interiority. Sketching is full, unconstrained attention to its occasion; it is
"BLOW[ing] AS DEEP" as one wants without concern for convention, market,
or "mysterious reader."

Two days after the first sketches, Kerouac announces, "I tell you today, Oct.
18, 1951, ON THE ROAD* TOOK OFF FROM THE GROUND."[27] The entry
shows that he was still thinking of this version as essentially a fictional narrative
(perhaps even what Latham terms "continuous narrative") and had yet to realize
how experimental (and lacking in conventional narrative) the *Cody* version of *On
the Road* would become. Moreover, the October 26 entry shows that he was still

thinking of the sketches as something separate from *Visions of Cody*, even though they would become its opening section. Still, the way Kerouac characterizes this new attempt reflects the impact of Kontiz's "I'll Remember April" performance, the exhortation of Newman to write as he talked, and the sense of writing as performance implicit in sketching:

> Wrote the great initial Dean Pomeray speech to Tom Watson & the football-passing scene in the Denver dusk & "great riot of October Joy" – a tremendous afternoon of writing. My new method is ACTING OUT what I write…SPEAKING OUT…(alone in the house) – and now of course don't need wire recorder no more – thank God – [28]

While here Kerouac stops short of characterizing writing as a system for recording speech, in his "new method" "ACTING" (imaginatively participating in the scene) occasions performing the scene as "SPEAKING," which eliminates the need for a wire or tape recorder. This suggests that Kerouac is here understanding writing as medium for recording "ACTING" and "SPEAKING" rather than an expressive system for composing. That he capitalizes "ACTING OUT" and "SPEAKING OUT" but not "write" also suggests that "ACTING" and "SPEAKING" are to be the actual creating, while writing, which presents them, is subordinate to them.

Kerouac's comments in the October 26 entry mark a further shift in his sense of narrative. Instead of narrative being primarily a matter of using fictional counters to present the "horizontal" of what happened or could have happened, narrative becomes something to be enacted – to be performed and recorded rather than to be composed. And acting here has its parallel in Method Acting (in the October 26 entry, he notes, "Mr. Stanislavski's advice…love the art in yourself"); the performing of narrative becomes inner discovery (or at least draws on what one finds in probing the self). This suggests that Kerouac, in "the football-passing scene," where he describes Cody and the boys he has just met at the pool hall tossing a football and bonding as they compete to make spectacular passes and catches, is not simply composing the scene nor simply representing the action. Instead, the scene intertwines the imagined October of the fictional moment with the actual October of Kerouac writing it, and these in turn intertwine with his memories of playing football (boyhood camaraderie and the October dusks that were part of those experiences). The "ACTING OUT" of the scene combines these frames into a single frame – the scene as performed by "SPEAKING OUT" what one is recovering, projecting, and transforming through "ACTING OUT," which is then stored in writing.

In this "new method," Kerouac's approach to the horizontal axis of narrative is already multilayered. The literal of what happened (or could have) is already "lyric-alto knowing," which substantially reduces the binary between "telled all" and the digressions of "lyric-alto knowing." Horizontal and vertical become complementary dimensions of a single process instead of two, conflicting alternatives. If sketching is in some sense the equivalent of "lyric-alto knowing" without regard for narrative, the "new method" for narrative Kerouac declares (and which he sees as the point of origin for *Visions of Cody* in the October 18 entry) paves the way for him to subsume narrative and digression, horizontal and vertical, into a single process – one which foregrounds performing and foregrounds the writer as a performer rather than a composer.

In this "new method," the imagined externality of the scene being narrated becomes both the occasion and the impetus for what Kerouac terms, in describing Konitz's performance, "interior music, the unspeakable visions of the individual." The elements of the situation and the action to occur become the equivalent of the song's structure and its harmonic system. The result is a performance of the self but not in a directly autobiographical sense, as the scene in *Visions of Cody* that immediately follows the "football-passing scene in the Denver dusk" illustrates. Cody and "the other fellows (Tom Watson, Slim Buckle, Earl Johnson)" (VC 71) come across "A whole bunch of sad and curious people and half morose" who are "kick[ing] around the weeds in the ordinary city debris of a field off East Avenue, Denver, October 1942, with semi-disgruntled expression that said 'There's something here anyway'" (VC 70). The scene next catalogues "Crap in weeds." The catalogue derives from one of the initial sketches from October 1951, which is included in a notebook (the pages approximately 2.5 by 6 inches) that Kerouac later labeled "Visions of Cody." At the top of the first page, he wrote.

> ON THE ROAD OCT. 1951
> A Modern Novel

Following a brief note about drinking and the figure of the "Shroudy Stranger," Kerouac then added:

> Now
> Blow as deep as
> You want to blow

The sketch, in pencil and two pages long, follows this exhortation:

Crap in Weeds

Old map,   Cashmere
soap paper, bottom glass
of a broken bottle, old
used-out flashlight battery, leaf,
torn small pages of news-
        (saw ???????)
paper, nameless cardboards,
nameless mats of hay,
light bulb cardboards, old
Spearmint gum wrappers,
ice cream box cover, old
paper bag, weeds with
little bunched lavender
shoots & Rousseaulike
but October rusted leaves—
old cellophane—old
bus transfer ticket, the
strange corrugated card-
board from egg crates,
a rock, pieces of
brown beerbottle glass,
old Philip Morris flattened
pack—the roots
of weeds just described
one purple borscht
color & leave the
matted filthy earth
like tormented dog
cocks leave the
sac—sticks—
coffee container—
& an empty pint
bottle of 4-Star
brand California sherry
drunk by the brakeman on a
night when things were less grim.[29]

In typing this sketch for *Visions of Cody* Kerouac ran the phrases (at least partly imposed by the narrowness of the notebook pages) as prose but preserved the original wording in almost all details. The most significant adjustment is to the final two lines, where "drunk by the brakeman on a / night when things were less grim" becomes "drunk by an old wino of the road when things were less grim."

The notebook version of the catalogue, which Kerouac apparently "sketched" while observing the actual scene, establishes that these observations were his own, not Cassady's somehow reported to Kerouac or ones that Kerouac invented for Cody, and the notebook version establishes that the scene occurred in New York in October 1951, not Denver in October 1942. The significance of this for Kerouac's "new method" becomes even clearer in the context of the October 13 work journal entry where he mentions Jerry Newman advising him to write like he "talked." Immediately lamenting, "If I had a tape-recorder everything would be okay…just walk and talk," he adds,

> Tonight I came upon a crowd in a field, with a cop in the middle, and a bloody hunk of human flesh in the weeds, apparently a miscarried baby dumped there, with a readleaf tree nearby framing a blue dusk moon. How strange – And wild little pickanninies screaming with glee, uncontrollably happy, outside a hardware store on Sutphin blvd.—The things I know don't last long anymore. They jump out of my head, I drink too much now… For the life and death of me I can't write ON THE ROAD…and I have to, I have to, or I'll just die off for God's sake.

In *Visions of Cody*, the catalogue of "Crap in weeds" leads immediately to "What actually had happened a miscarriage was discovered by some children in the field" (VC 70), and this triggers a meditation on sexuality and mortality, which concludes, "Thus Cody ponders. Whatever he says (in the tragic dusk of this field, bareheaded), he says nothing now – " (VC 71).

The scene with the miscarriage is probably not the same scene that occasions "Crap in Weeds." The latter seems a daytime scene, and it is unlikely that Kerouac would have pulled out his notebook to catalogue the "Crap" as he stood in a crowd confronted with "a miscarried baby dumped there." The scene in *Visions of Cody* is, then, an amalgam of moments, not a single moment. Moreover, Kerouac presents the material not as his own experience but as Cody's (as if Kerouac in narrating the scene is retelling something Cody has told him). In a sense Kerouac here is merely doing what all fiction writers do: constructing what they write for their characters by drawing on their own experience. But the way Kerouac uses the details of the "Crap in Weeds" sketch to intensify the reader's (and his own) awareness of the actual setting for the miscarried fetus (details probably not visible in the dark) drives a meditation that, while ostensibly Cody's interior musings, is actually Kerouac exploring his reactions through the mediation of his character. In the scene, Kerouac does not use his own experiences to create Cody; he creates Cody (out of his impressions of Cassady, bits of Cassady's history, and himself) to engage his own experience through Cody, much as Konitz (as Kerouac understood it) had engaged and performed his interiority through "I'll Remember April." In this scene, Cody and his buddies encountering the milling crowd are the material to be performed, and Kerouac performs his own interiority through the externalized figure of Cody.

Precisely when Kerouac wrote (i.e., performed in writing) the scene where Cody and his football buddies encounter the miscarriage is unclear, but the November 14 journal entry offers a further gloss on how he probably wrote it. Kerouac begins the entry noting that he's "on the verge of some kind of crazy discovery" that will either "make me great" or mark the failure of the experiments he'd been attempting since the April 1951 scroll:

> The system of writing I use when sketching is tranced fixation on an object before me, "dreaming on it" expresses it exactly; now I'm about to try the most dangerous experiment of my life, the same tranced unconscious fixation upon the object which will now be the successive chronological visions of Neal, in other words, I'll decide ahead of time generally where he's at, with who, what doing, and dream on it. As in the sketches, as in all portraiture, present tense.

Kerouac, here, sets himself the task of writing narrative, "Fiction," by "sketching." That is, he proposes erasing the distinction between sketching as something done for himself and his "main ms." as something done for the reader, which is in turn to say that Kerouac here proposes writing narrative as a series of performances, something he had been edging toward from the initial experiments in trying to write his "confession" through writing letters to Cassady in late December 1950. That Kerouac recognized how much writing narrative by sketching would further compromise publishing his work is clear in his final comment before breaking off the entry to commence the experiment: "It's 4 A.M. in the morning and I am about to try the experiment & I'm scared."

The continuation of the entry, after the "experiment," does not indicate what Kerouac had just written, but clearly he believed he had proved what he'd set out to prove:

> IT WORKED—but I would have written it in huge letters if I was positive it would work when the time comes dialog, for voices of others. Generally speaking, it works and I can report here, as if I was an inventor at his peak,

that I've gone still another greater step beyond the fruits of the hospital discoveries…and I knew this was so, because I couldn't sleep the night I first realized it Oct. 25, the day I wrote the Bowery sketch from memory [see VC, pp.6-8, for the passage Kerouac probably refers to here] realizing that I was in myself revolutionizing writing by removing literary & that curious "literary-grammatical" inhibition from its moment of inception, removing most of all, of course, the obstacles that came from my own personal stupidity which is still with me but temporarily under control.

Even though Kerouac admits that he is not yet sure how to use this approach for dialogue between figures within the fiction (as opposed to his own implicit dialogue with the fiction), he clearly believes he has just demonstrated that narrative can be sketched (performed) instead of only composed. This not only reduces the conflict between his desire to sketch and his need to work on his "main ms.," it also alters what he can address in the "main ms." In the passage quoted above, the phrase "temporarily under control" is followed by "(And someday must tell the strangest tale of tonight's discovery which is actually going to influence my entire life and yet I'm not excited and why should I be – the scatological block I had, the fear of soiling bound notebooks no matter how small.)," suggests that the experiment could have been the scene where Cody and the gang come upon the crowd and that miscarriage dumped in the weeds. If not, Kerouac's sense that he has found a way to remove "obstacles" (whether the expected rhetoric of literary fiction, conventional grammar, or "personal stupidity") makes possible the passage where he meditates, through Cody, on the "miscarried whatnot":

But now: what a forlorn thing it is and frightening that the nameless soul (the thing created by the terribleness of a womb which when it does halfway work or even complete work takes the melted marble of a man's sperm which is a kind of acceptable substance, say in a bottle, and transforms it by means of the work of some heinous secret egg into a large bulky piece of decayable meat—) that this nameless little would-have-been lay, spilling out of that grocer's bag, grocer's wrapping, under a tree that by dry Autumn had been turned almost the same shade of red, turned thus instead of by wet and secret wombs—Girls are frightening when you see them under these circumstances because there seems to be a kind of insistence on their part to look you in the eye to find out that personal thing about you which is probably the thing that you expect and burn and kill to find in them when you think of penetrating their thighs—that secret wetness of the woman is as unknown to you as your eyes are to her when they're confronted by a miscarried whatnot in a field under dark and mortal

> skies—Thus Cody ponders. Whatever he says (in the tragic dusk of this
> field, bareheaded), he says nothing now— .(VC 71)

This passage seemingly illustrates what Latham has in mind when he declares that *Visions of Cody* is "bits and pieces," not "a continuous narrative." However, the passage illustrates the way imagined and recalled "bits" of narrative generate reflective responses and how these responses in turn elicit further "bits" of imagined and recalled narrative.[30] The scene, that is, enacts what Kerouac terms the "horizontal" and the "vertical" in tandem, as part of a single action. In the scene, "lyric-alto knowing" is integral to the fiction rather than outside it or opposed to it. While *Visions of Cody* lacks a single line of action at the level of plot, its "bits and pieces" are interwoven strands to be read in relationship to each other.

In the fall 1951 work journal, Kerouac mentions nearly all the sketches and scenes in Parts 1 and 2 of *Visions of Cody*, which suggests that he had the initial drafts of this material in hand by November 25 (the date of the last entry) before leaving for San Francisco, where he lived with Neal Cassady for the rest of the winter and through spring of 1952 as he wrote the material in Part 3 of *Cody*. The pool hall scene that opens Part 2 (VC 47-56), apparently written September 18, seems the earliest unit in *Visions of Cody* and is probably the only piece drafted as a possible "insertion" for the April 1951 scroll. The rest of Parts 1 and 2 dates from early October through late November, some of it initially generated as notebook sketches that Kerouac later sequenced and adapted as he put the book together (presumably while in San Francisco); some of it narrative bits about Cody's boyhood in Denver from the "main ms." that was for a time to replace the April 1951 scroll; and some of it sketches and sketched narrative written after Kerouac determined that he would combine the initial sketches with scenes done for the "main ms.," then use sketching to write the rest of the *Cody* version of *On the Road*.

By mid-November, Kerouac had, the entries show, committed fully to sketching as *the* method for writing works of fiction (not just for writing independent pieces for himself). They also show that he had determined to write a sketched version of *On the Road* (i.e., *Visions of Cody*) but that he was still worried that this would undercut his ability to publish and earn money through his writing. In the November 15 entry, he asserts, "From now on when I say 'write' I therefore mean 'sketch,'" but two days later he was debating whether to "finish" what he terms the "Dean road first" (i.e., finish reworking the April scroll) or to "go to sea." The pairing suggests that he saw revising the scroll at this point, at least in part, as a way to make enough money to be able to focus on writing *Cody*:

Goddamit I want to use the Proustian method of recollection and amazement but <u>as I go along</u> in life, not after, so therefore why don't I allow myself to write about Neal and using his real name in my own private scribble book for my own joy!—doesn't my own work& joy belong to me any more?

<u>IF I DON'T DO THIS, I LIE</u> —Tonite's "work" consisted of nothing but expositions about "Dean" for the "reader" [squiggled line, then a sentence in French, with Kerouac's translation in square brackets following: Here's what I wrote—"Of course Dean immediately conned the whole gang, Bill Johnson who was the central golden boy before him, Al Buckle the real pillar..." —what mincing camping crap]—and I have a real tragic actual Neal in my thoughts all the time that I repress for this kind of coal, here I am with a real mind & won't use it. If I can't begin tonight I simply never will—that's all. The real, the real, afraid of the real—Oh Jesus forgive me—Teach me to write "for your own future reference"—If I were in Istanbul tonight wouldn't it be best to fill an entire notebook with the things that I see in front of me, & with visions of what I see plus whatever haunted hangup was underway (say my relation to ship or what not) instead of...some dumb story or other. The story is the echo chamber of my own rain maybe...let me tell the story of right now...but if I do, completely, I might get to Neal via the honest way. Oh help me!—

Six days later, Kerouac wrote a long letter to Cassady (incorporated into *Visions of Cody* as the conclusion of Part 1) announcing that he was coming to San Francisco.

While Kerouac's dilemma with *Visions of Cody* was partly economic, it was also partly conceptual. How to handle "dialog, for voices of others" in sketching was, as he recognized in the November 14 entry, one challenge, perhaps because inventing dialogue seemed to involve considering the eventual ("mysterious") reader in a way that sketching a physical scene or memory need not. And as such, dialogue seemed to require composing, not performance. The other challenge was how to integrate sketches that had been performed as separate pieces into the larger whole of a book, a work of "Fiction." Selecting and arranging sketches, like composing dialogue, required thinking of the sketched pieces as units within a larger, pre-determined design that would, at least to some extent, be shaped with the reader's expectation in mind. Kerouac's sense that the "'what happened next'" of what occurs in the book should be derived from the writer's participation in the material (not the reader's expectation) is implicit in the first of two journal entries for November 15: "The secret of 'what happened next' is not a narrative secret but merely what the teller genuinely hung-uply wants to explain & unfold next about the subject he's on, whether it's action or a turd." And the November

16 entry shows his sense that using plotted action to structure what he was trying to develop in *Cody* would not work:

> Made important decision about the Neal book [i.e., the *Visions of Cody* version of *On the Road*]—no false action, just visions of what I know he did, NO TIME, NO CHRONOLOGY, composing willy-nilly, as Holmes says, a book surpassing the problem of time by itself being full of the roar of Time (not his words).

To erase "TIME" to replace it with "Time" might seem oxymoronic, even inane. However, Kerouac is recognizing a crucial implication of his sketching (i.e., Spontaneous Prose) aesthetic: That plot, in the conventional sense, involves constructing representations of "time" for the "reader" and that represented "time" cannot be actual time for either the writer or the reader, because in such a system and process neither writer nor reader engage actual time (i.e., the diachronic action of time elapsing, which Kittler terms "data flow"). The written work is a systematized structure of words, but its relationship to actual time, elapsing time, is necessarily structural and symbolic rather than involving a direct correspondence between the act of writing as time, time within and through the writing, and the act of reading as a process in time. "Time" represented for the reader cannot be actual time for either the writer or reader because it is not a matter of engaging time and not a matter of acting within it.[31] As such, represented "time" is disconnected not only from the actual unfolding of time that the plot purports to enact (but only represents) but also from the actual unfolding of the time of the composing (both in the sense of "when" and in the sense of "how long"). From one aesthetic perspective (the typical critical perspective?), represented time is, thus, doubly redeemed – saved from the mere actuality of its production and raised above the mere actuality of events within the flow of actual time. From Kerouac's perspective, as he discovered his way into the *Cody* version of *On the Road*, represented or constructed time was, instead, doubly false. To write by sketching, the sketching writer had to operate within "time" and enact it, and the writing of the sketch had to record (not symbolize) that process directly. Rather than represent "time" (which is to replace it), to sketch is to record "time" (the timing and elapsing of time during the performance that is its making) in writing and through writing.

To erase the represented or constructed "TIME" of "CHRONOLOGY" (either invented for the fiction or selected from recalled events) is to make space on the page and within the writing process to replace the "problem" of composing "TIME" with the possibility of performing within time (sketching), which (when recorded) allows the sketch to enact time. And this in turn allows the sketching writer, the sketch as a recording of its sketching, and the reader of / listener to the sketch to participate in "the roar of Time." In this entry, Kerouac recognizes that his experiments of the fall involve a different aesthetic, a different sense of what writing should be, than the scroll *On the Road*. He also recognizes a key aspect of the problem he still needed to solve: how to combine sketched performances (each necessarily relatively brief and rooted in the sketcher's immediate interest in the material, not the sketch's later function in the larger set that would be the book) into a work of "Fiction" without falsifying the original performance by replacing the actuality of time with a structure symbolizing time.

In the journal's final entry Kerouac clearly assumes that he will be able to adapt the sketching aesthetic to produce a new *On the Road* (i.e., *Visions of Cody*) that would be the "roar of Time" rather than a composed representation of it:

> Something that you feel will find its own form. That's all there is to it. So, after a 1½ mile walk, I started on <u>the redbrick wall behind the neons</u> to prove this & begin my-life-alone-in-America: I'm lost, but my work is found. Last night there was a face in my window, saying "Write what you want." I thought it was Faulkner, I think it was really Dr. Sax. I'm going to write over 3000 words a day like this and see what I have at Xmas.

> So the growing peace, and the most beautiful visions of life that began three months ago & which were great enough for a Remembrance 10,000,000 words long, the peace has led to mind filled with work and a soul fortified with the knowledge of the inevitability of loss—and so goodbye sweet journal, adieu calm book, may the best hearts find you.

Whatever the hesitations, shifts in terms, second thoughts, and temporary changes in direction it documents, Kerouac's fall 1951 work journal establishes that he developed sketching (what he later labeled Spontaneous Prose) out of his dissatisfaction with the April 1951 scroll version of *On the Road*, that he initially thought of sketching as a practice separate from the fiction he was trying to write at that point and the question of what to do with *On the Road*, but that he then committed himself as the fall went on – partly in response to what he took to be Lee Konitz's approach in performing "I'll Remember April," partly in response to the advice from Jerry Newman that he write like he talked, and partly from his experiments with sketching – to working out a mode of fiction in which he would generate the material to become the book by performing in writing (sketching) rather than composing in writing.

But if this final entry indicates *what* Kerouac wants *Cody* to be, it also suggests that he had yet to work out how to use sketches and sketching for structuring a book as opposed to generating its pieces. The challenge was not simply to find a way to write so that the writing would function for the reader as action in time rather than an object outside of time but how to direct and structure such writing for an extended work of "Fiction" without falsifying the process being used to generate the units of writing to be included. In Kerouac's initial practice of sketching in fall 1951, as contextualized by his fall 1951 work journal and the other manuscript material from the period, sketching provided a procedure for writing but not a procedure for combining sketches into an extended work of "Fiction." It pointed toward a work of fiction that would be "'soulwork'" but did not provide a map for getting there. Sketching resolved the problem of "the mysterious reader" for individual sketches but "the mysterious reader" was still a problem for Kerouac when it came to organizing a book. The material Kerouac gathered as Part 3 of *Visions of Cody* and the way Kerouac, in the spring of 1952, wove together the *Visions of Cody* typescript reflect the route, the specific writerly road, he discovered as he expanded the logic of sketching into the more comprehensive practice of Spontaneous Prose.

Notes

[1]   This essay is drawn from a work in progress, *Textual Subversion: Kerouac and the Advent of Post-Literary Literature*. The initial pages are from the Introduction, the remainder from Chapter 4, a consideration of the drafting of Parts 1 and 2 of *Visions of Cody*. In *Textual Subversion*, this discussion of the drafting of Parts 1 and 2 is followed by a chapter that considers Kerouac's experimenting in Part 3 with tape recording in "Frisco: The Tape" and "Imitation of the Tape" and how these experiments diverge from, and then reconnect with, the experiments with sketching and Spontaneous Prose in Parts 1 and 2.

[2]   Ong, Goody, Havelock, and others who have engaged the literacy hypothesis have tended to focus on how historical transitions from orality to literacy can clarify the nature of writing as a mode of language. Investigations into how oral language itself developed have not, in general, been part of this research agenda, but work in this area can provide a productive, if speculative, complement to analyses of the transitions from orality to literacy. The work of the cognitive psychologist Merlin Donald, the microsociologist Jonathan H. Turner, and others who consider language in an evolutionary context have rich implications for understanding how speaking differs from writing.

[3]   In *The Power of the Written Tradition,* Jack Goody offers a cogent review of the work he and others have done on the literacy hypothesis and also addresses attacks on the position.

4   See "Men Talking in Bars," included in *Kerouac's Crooked Road: Development of a Fiction.*

5   The research connected to the literacy hypothesis has had its greatest impact for those interested in verbal performance traditions that flourished prior to writing and works from cultures in transition from (to use Ong's terminology) "orality" to "literacy." In fact, Milman Parry's research into the composition and performance of the Homeric epics remains foundational, as does the research he and Albert Lord initiated that evolved into Lord's *The Singer of Tales.* See John Miles Foley's *The Theory of Oral Composition: History and Methodology* for a succinct, insightful review of overview this field.

6   "The There That's There and Not There in the Writing of Writing: Textuality and Modern American Poetry" and "Showing vs. Telling: Toward a Rhetoric of the Page" explore this application of Vachek for considering poetry (including "In a Station of the Metro") and are posted at www.tahunt.com. The distinction between "composing" and "performing," which figures in this discussions is the focus of my essay "The Muse Learns to Tape," in *Reimagining Textuality: Textual Studies in the Late Age of Print.*

7   Jerome McGann, Peter Shillingsburg, John Bryant, and George Bornstein are among those who have, in various ways, significantly contributed to our understanding of what McGann has termed "the textual condition."

8   *Windblown World* (95).

9   Originally *The New York Times Book Review*, January 28, 1973: http://www.nytimes.com/books/97/09/07/home/kerouac-cody.html.

10   Holmes quoted from this letter in *Nothing More to Declare* (80). It is not included in Ann Charters' edition of Kerouac's letters but will, hopefully, be included in the edition of Kerouac's and Holmes' correspondence that is in preparation.

11   This point is covered at some length in *Kerouac's Crooked Road* (120-142).

12   *Windblown World* (95) For a discussion of this entry, see Chapter Two, *Textual Subversion* (forthcoming).

13   Speech-act theory, as initiated by J. L. Austin, further explored by John Searle, and adapted and developed for literary studies by Mary Louise Pratt, offers in many ways a productive and powerful approach to understanding the presence of spoken dynamics within writing, but Kerouac's apparent need, in developing Spontaneous Prose, to move beyond using writing to represent speech and instead to search for a way to have writing function as if speaking points, I would suggest, to an inherent limitation of speech-act theory. Writing can be used to construct representations of "utterance" but writing is not "uttering." To write (at least in the usual sense) is to construct a text for later retrieval often under unspecified conditions at an unknown time. To speak is to interact directly with

another; it is interactive behavior. By drawing on aspects of oral rhetoric based in speaking's interactivity, speech-act theory can account for some of the oddities of how writing works, but it does not fully confront the nature of depth of the differences between speaking and writing as media. Both Ong and Kittler offer more productive ways of engaging these differences, and these differences are precisely what matter for considering Spontaneous Prose.

[14] *Selected Letters, Vol.* 1 (315). Subsequent citations noted parenthetically as SL.

[15] The Jack Kerouac Archive, The Henry W. and Albert A. Berg Collection of English and American Literature, The New York Public Library, holds two typescripts of *On the Road*. The earlier of the two is perhaps the one Kerouac prepared from the scroll.

[16] Kerouac to Holmes, July 14, 1951.

[17] *Excerpts from Visions of Cody* New Directions: New York, 1960 (this note was not assigned a page number).

[18] *On the Road* as published by Viking does, actually, include moments of what might be termed "lyric-alto knowing" written as Spontaneous Prose, and these are often the passages cited when praising Kerouac's writing in the book. These passages were, however, added for the most part probably no earlier than 1954 and as late as 1956, well after Kerouac had written *Visions of Cody*, as Ryan J. Ehmke, drawing on manuscript material in the Jack Kerouac Archive, has demonstrated in his master's thesis, "Unravelling the Scroll: A Fluid-Text Analysis of Kerouac's Road" (August 2009, Illinois State University).

[19] This would, that is, have made *On the Road* more like *The Great Gatsby*, but in making Sal more like Nick, it would have undercut what he had accomplished in the scroll.

[20] Ann Charters, *Jack Kerouac: A Bibliography* (17).

[21] The quotations from this work journal are cited by the date of the entry. The journal is item 55.6 of the Jack Kerouac Archive, where it is listed as "Holograph notebook '1951 / Journals / More Notes.' August 28, 1951 – November 25, 1951."

[22] See "The Essentials of Spontaneous Prose" for Kerouac's later codification of sketching as Spontaneous Prose.

[23] See *Visions of Cody* (69-70).

[24] From item 30.1, "Holograph notebook 'Visions of Cody' / 'Visions of Neal,'" dated October 1951, Jack Kerouac Archive. The breaks in the transcription reflect the margin of the notebook pages.

[25] George Dardess also discusses this sketch in "The Logic of Spontaneity" (736-737). Dardess stresses that the sketcher's eye "imposes no subordination on the objects it lovingly occupies," so that the "worlds of mind and matter are view with an equal degree of fascination and delight," which culminates "in

the 'release' phase of 'spontaneous prose.'" Dardess persuasively correlates the sketch to "Essential of Spontaneous Prose," but he perhaps doesn't fully acknowledge the extent to which the "I" of the sketcher, what might be thought of as the sketcher's situated subjectivity, complicates the work of the sketching "eye" so that the action of the sketch is not only perceptual but also social and psychological. The difference in emphasis between his reading and mine is also a matter of context. The occasion for Dardess' analysis is the sketch, in revised and slightly extended form, as it appears as the opening passage of *Visions of Cody* rather than the scene as first sketched as a discrete piece in Kerouac's notebook.

26 The role that Kerouac's access to Jerry Newman's studio and awareness of Newman's work recording jazz musicians played in Kerouac's development of *On the Road* and *Visions of Cody* deserves fuller study. It should also be noted here that Kerouac did experiment with tape recording in Part 3 of *Visions of Cody*, in the section titled "Frisco: The Tape," a primary focus of the fifth chapter of the book from which this essay derives. For discussions of Kerouac's experimenting with tape recording in Part 3 of *Visions of Cody*, see James Riley's "'I am a Recording Angel': Jack Kerouac's *Visions of Cody* and the Recording Process" and John Shapcott's "'I Didn't Punctuate It": Locating the Tape and Text of Jack Kerouac's *Visions of Cody* and *Doctor Sax* in a Culture of Spontaneous Improvisation." Both Riley and Shapcott develop important points about Kerouac's use of the tape recorder. They underestimate, I believe, the extent to which Kerouac experienced writing and speaking as different, even conflicting ways of practicing language and how this shaped his approach to tape recording and its implications for Spontaneous Prose.

27 When Kerouac reviewed this journal at some later date, he added an asterisk after "ON THE ROAD" and wrote at the bottom of the page "(*VISIONS OF CODY....later title)."

28 This presumably refers to pp. 50-70 of *VC* as published.

29 Item 30.1, The Kerouac Archive.

30 For a discussion of how this scene interacts with the scenes that precede and follow it, see *Kerouac's Crooked Road* (148-154).

31 See Friedrich Kittler's Introduction to *Gramphone, Typewriter, Film.*

Acknowledgments

Jack Kerouac's fall 1951 work journal and the notebook that includes the original drafts of the "Old Diner" and "Crap in Weeds" are both part of the Jack Kerouac Archive of The Henry W. and Albert A. Berg Collection of English and American Literature of the New York Public Library. The quotations from these materials appear here with the kind permission of the Estate of Stella Kerouac, John Sampas, Literary Representative and The Henry W. and Albert A. Berg Collection of English and American Literature. These documents are central to this essay, and I thank Mr. Sampas for his generosity in extending permission to quote. I would also like to thank Dr. Isaac Gewirtz, Curator of The Henry W. and Albert A. Berg Collection of English and American Literature, for his thoughtful guidance and his support of this project.

Works Cited and Consulted

Bornstein, George. *Material Modernism: The Politics of the Page*. NY: Cambridge UP, 2001.

Bryant, John. *The Fluid Text: A Theory of Revision for Editing for Book and Screen*. Ann Arbor, MI: University of Michigan Press, 2002.

Charters, Ann. *Jack Kerouac: A Bibliography* (Rev. Ed.). NY: The Phoenix Bookshop, 1975.

Dardess, George, "The Logic of Spontaneity: A Reconsideration of Kerouac's 'Spontaneous Prose Method.'" *Boundary 2* 3.3 (1975): pp. 729-743.

Donald, Merlin. *Origins of the Modern Mind: Three Stages in the Evolution of Culture and Cognition*. Cambridge, MA: Harvard UP, 1991.

Ehmke, Ryan J. "Unravelling the Scroll: A Fluid-Text Analysis of Kerouac's Road." (Unpublished Master's Thesis, August 2009, Illinois State University).

Foley, John Miles. *The Theory of Oral Composition: History and Methodology*. Bloomington, IN: Indiana UP, 1988.

Goody, Jack. *The Power of the Written Tradition*. Washington, D.C.: Smithsonian Institution P, 2000.

Grace, Nancy M. *Jack Kerouac and the Literary Imagination*. NY: Palgrave Macmillan, 2009.

Havelock, Eric A. *The Muse Learns to Write: Reflections on Orality and Literacy from Antiquity to the Present*. New Haven, CT: Yale UP, 1986.

Holmes, John Clellon. *Nothing More to Declare*. NY: E.P. Dutton, 1967,

Hrebeniak, Michael. *Action Writing: Jack Kerouac's Wild Form*. Carbondale, IL: Southern Illinois UP, 2006.

Hunt, Tim. *Kerouac's Crooked Road: The Development of a Fiction*. Carbondale, IL: Southern Illinois University Press, 2010.

---. "The Muse Learns to Tape." *Reimagining Textuality: Textual Studies in the Late Age of Print*, Ed. Elizabeth Loizeaux and Neil Fraistat. Madison, WI: U of Wisconsin P, 2002. 189-210.

Johnson, Ronna. "'You're putting me on': Jack Kerouac and the Postmodern Emergence" *College Literature* 27.1 (2000): pp. 22-38.

Kerouac, Jack. *Excerpts from Visions of Cody.* NY: New Directions, 1960.

---. "Essentials of Spontaneous Prose." *Evergreen Review* 2.5 (1958): pp. 72-73. Reprinted in *The Portable Beat Reader*, Ed. Ann Charters. NY: Penguin Books, 1992: pp. 57-58.

---. *On the Road.* NY: Viking Press, 1957. Reprinted Penguin, 1976.

---. *Selected Letters 1940-1956*, Ed. Ann Charters. NY: Penguin, 1995.

---. *Visions of Cody.* NY: McGraw-Hill, 1972.

---. *Windblown World: The Journals of Jack Kerouac 1947-1954*, Ed. Douglas Brinkley. NY: Viking, 2004.

Kittler, Friedrich. *Gramophone, Film, Typewriter.* Stanford, CA: Stanford UP, 1999.

Latham, Aaron. "*Visions of Cody.*" Rev. of *Visions of Cody* by Jack Kerouac. *The New York Times Book Review*, 28 January 1973 (http://www.nytimes.com/books/97/09/07/home/kerouac-cody.html).

McGann, Jerome. *The Textual Condition.* Princeton, NJ: Princeton UP, 1991.

Ong, Walter. *Orality and Literacy: The Technologizing of the Word.* NY: Routledge, 2002.

Riley, James. "'I am a Recording Angel': Jack Kerouac's *Visions of Cody* and the Recording Process." *Electronic Book Review* (2006) (http://www.electronicbookreview.com/thread/musicsoundnoise/angelic).

Shapcott, John. "'I Didn't Punctuate It': Locating the Tape and Text of Jack Kerouac's *Visions of Cody* and *Doctor Sax* in a Culture of Spontaneous Improvisation." *Journal of American Studies* 36.2 (2002): pp. 231-248.

Shillingsburg, Peter. *Resisting Texts: Authority and Submission in Constructions of Meaning.* Ann Arbor, MI: U of Michigan P, 1997.

Tallman, Warren, "Kerouac's Sound." *The Tamarack Review* Spring (1959): pp. 58-74. Reprinted in *A Casebook on the Beat*, Ed. Thomas Parkinson. NY: Thomas Y. Crowell, 1961: pp. 215-229.

Theado, Matt. *Understanding Jack Kerouac.* Columbia, SC: U of South Carolina P, 2000.

Turner, Jonathan H. *On the Origins of Human Emotions: A Sociological Inquiry into the Evolution of Human Affect.* Stanford, CA: Stanford UP, 2000.

Tytell, John. *Naked Angels: The Lives and Literature of the Beat Generation.* NY: McGraw-Hill, 1976.

Vachek, Josef. *Written Language Revisited.* Philadelphia: John Benjamins, 1989.

Weinreich, Regina. *Kerouac's Spontaneous Prose: A Study of the Fiction.* Carbondale, IL: Southern Illinois UP, 1987.

Reviews

Sutras & Bardos: Essays & Interviews on Allen Ginsberg, the Kerouac School, Anne Waldman, The Postbeat Poets & the New Demotics. Jim Cohn (Boulder, CO: Museum of American Poetics Publications, 2011)

It is a cliché, of course, to say "the Beats go on." For several decades now, cultural critics, biographers, and reviewers have echoed the cry "the Beats go on." Behind the banner newspaper headlines and the slick magazine stories about the Beats and their cultural descendants, there is an unmistakable germ of truth. On blogs, as well as in bookstores, bohemian haunts, and college classrooms, the writers of the Beat Generations—plural—go on and on and on with little sign of diminution or atrophy. Perhaps no one in the United States today understands and appreciates the poetic durability and the cultural elasticity of the Beats better than Jim Cohn, the author of *Sutras & Bardos: Essays & Interviews on Allen Ginsberg, the Kerouac School, Anne Waldman, The Postbeat Poets & the New Demotics.*

Born in Highland Park, Illinois in 1953—three years before the publication of *Howl*, four years before the publication of *On the Road*—Cohn came of age in the aftermath of the initial flowering of the first wave of Beat Generation writers in the mid-1950s. Old enough to have experienced the 1960s, and yet young enough to have been shaped early in life by the development of digital technology and the computer, he is a pivotal figure linking generations and schools of thought.

Drawn almost instinctively to Allen Ginsberg's poetry and to his personality, Cohn studied with Ginsberg at the Jack Kerouac School of Disembodied Poetics at Naropa University in Boulder, Colorado, and worked as his teaching assistant in 1980. Ginsberg has been a lifelong influence on Cohn's poetry, his teaching, and his sense of citizenship, along with pivotal figures such as Anne Waldman, Amiri Baraka, and a slew of other poets from Walt Whitman and Ezra Pound to Ted Berrigan. Cohn pays homage to these figures in his new, refreshing book that brings together twenty essays and five interviews, many of them previously published in journals and reviews such as *Logos*, *The Arts Paper* and *Paterson Literary Review* and newly revised for inclusion in *Sutras & Bardos*.

Cohn's book has several distinctive characteristics that make it appealing, and even compelling, reading. It is intensely personal and deeply autobiographical with the author's own dreams, reflections, and journeys in search of poetry, poets, and the poetic. "In Valparaiso, I visited Pablo Neruda's home, high on a steep hillside," Cohn writes in an essay on the 150th anniversary of the publication of *Leaves of Grass* (24). At the same time, *Sutras & Bardos* is profoundly theoretical. "Form is an extension of *emptiness*," the author writes. "Poems take place in a space nothing can fill" (21). Elsewhere, he notes that literary movements have "*porosity*, or openness, such that certain poets are viewed interchangeably" (172).

Scholars and students of the Beats will probably find his terms useful, though they may also find some of them, such as "porosity," new and perhaps even unusual. Cohn always defines his terms. Sutras, he explains in the introduction to the book, are "a distinct Eastern literary form that employs minimal syllabary and is unambiguous, pithy, comprehensive, continuous and without flaw." Bardos, he adds, are "the intermediate or intimate transitional or in-between or liminal states after death and before one's next birth." There is plenty of food for thought here.

Cohn is also generous in his appreciations of writers, including his own contemporaries and near contemporaries such as Eileen Myles, Ingrid Swanberg, David Cope, Gary Gach, Marc Olmstead, Eliot Katz, and Antler, the pen name for Brad Burdick, the author of *Factory*, published by City Lights, and a former poet laureate of Milwaukee whom Ginsberg described as "one of Whitman's poets and orators to come."

"Poetry comes from all over the world in all times from all peoples," Cohn writes (58). Moreover, he has produced a book with real verve and with poetic language that resonates from beginning to end and with provocative ideas on nearly every page. In the essay, "Embodying Knowledge (Robo-Mona Lisa, An Allegory)," he writes about the "*promiscuous rubbish* of the present" (7). It is a phrase that demonstrates how well he learned from Ginsberg, especially Ginsberg's ability to coin phrases like "hydrogen jukebox." "Promiscuous rubbish" comes from the same brand of imagination as "hydrogen jukebox."

In *Sutras & Bardos*, there are insights into the private lives of Ginsberg, Waldman, Berrigan, and others, as teachers and as poets, and revelations about the intimate world of poetry at Naropa. Cohn manages to appreciate *When I Was Cool*, a memoir meant to shock readers about sex and drugs at Naropa. He even manages to make kindly comments about the author, Sam Kashner, who aimed to expose the flaws of Ginsberg and crew. "In a way, he was dead-on about those days," Cohn writes of Kashner. "You could live to regret ever having stepped out of your world and into those of the poetics faculty" (41). Heroes abound in this book, but it does not offer unalloyed hero worship.

Granted, Cohn writes about the night in 1975 when the Buddhist monk Trungpa Rinpoche ordered the poet W.S. Merwin and his companion, Dana Naone, to take off their clothes at Naropa, an incident that became a "cause célèbre among poets and artists" (174). *Sutras & Bardos* is not, however, a compilation of outrageous behaviors, regrets, and misgivings. Cohn is not out to unmask the famous and the infamous, but rather to offer a portrait of a sustainable and sustaining community that was rooted at Naropa and that moved about the country, from Wisconsin to New York and beyond.

The essays and interviews in *Sutras & Bardos* are overtly political. Cohn believes and even insists that the Beats and the Postbeats must be understood in the context of their time and place: the original Beats in the context of the cold war and McCarthyism, and the Postbeats in the context of the War on Terror and "androidization," which he defines as "the transformation of humans into machines" (5). Cohn is a partisan, not a disinterested spectator. Like Ginsberg, he is a foe of all kinds of tyranny and a defender of "underground or suppressed cultures" (77). But he does not offer propaganda, and even about his favorite crowd, the poets of the world, he has a balanced perspective. "Poets are not the most social people," he explains in an interview that Rob Geisen conducted with him in 2008. He adds, "In fact, they do their best socializing in poems" (75).

Cohn uses the format of the interview effectively. His voice is almost always informal and conversational, even when he is talking about bardos, androidization, and porosity, and especially in the interviews with him. In the last interview in the book, conducted with Randy Roark, Cohn includes one of his own poems, "George Washington Bridge, Lower Level, Clear Day," writing clearly and candidly about its origins and development. An insightful critic of his own work, he explains that "George Washington Bridge, Lower Level, Clear Day" was for him "like Walt Whitman on LSD."

Cohn mostly does not draw attention to himself nor promote himself. For him, the Postbeats are post-narcissistic and post-egoistic. They are not out to seek self-aggrandizement. But he does honor his own contributions, and while he reveals the influences of Ginsberg on his own work, he also describes his influences on his teacher and mentor. In 1984, he introduced Ginsberg to an audience of deaf poets—an experience that did not irrevocably transform Ginsberg but shaped him in subtle ways.

If there is one essay in the book in which Cohn crystallizes his thinking it is "Postbeat Transcendence," written in 2010, in which he argues that "Revolutionary spiritual pluralism is a core element on Postbeat literature" and that Postbeat poets address "sacredness of place and natural resources" (119, 129). Of course, some of the characteristics that Cohn ascribes to the Postbeats can also be found in the original Beats. Ginsberg, Kerouac, and Snyder all appreciated the sacredness of place—the sacredness of America itself—and the value of natural resources.

Sutras & Bardos does not end the discussion of what it means to be a Postbeat writer. Cohn's comments about Bob Dylan and Patti Smith, for example, which appear in "Postbeat Transcendence," only scratch the surface of the subject. But here as in Michael McClure's seminal work, *Scratching the Beat Surface*, Cohn's cultural, historical, and intellectual scratching of the Postbeat surface goes a long way toward creating an understanding of a literary movement that has broken new ground even as it has continued on the original path carved out by Kerouac, Ginsberg, Snyder—and McClure, too, who read at the 6 Gallery in 1955, participated in the Human Be-In in 1967, and who is at the age of 79 still writing and still proof that the Beats do go on and on and on.

---Jonah Raskin, *Sonoma State University*

East Hill Farm: Seasons with Allen Ginsberg.
Gordon Ball (Berkeley, CA: Counterpoint, 2011)

Any Allen Ginsberg scholar is aware of Gordon Ball's already considerable contributions, specifically his *Allen Verbatim*, literally the first collection of interviews, and his intelligent editing of two volumes of Ginsberg's journals. In *East Hill Farm: Seasons with Allen Gisnberg*, Ball explains how Ginsberg, founder and treasurer of the Committee on Poetry, Inc., funded an intentional "haven for comrades in distress" in the late 1960s. Thus, the East Hill Farm came to be.

Ginsberg's resultant upstate New York Cherry Valley farm has come up in three biographies and is documented in his collection of poetry *Fall of America*. Still, this 1967-1970 period usually gets passed over quickly because of the sheer density of Ginsberg's life-material. What a pleasure to see this section of Ginsberg's life "slowed down" into a 400-plus page book, all the more so because Gordon Ball actually lived there. To quote Ginsberg's own words from the back cover of *East Hill Farm*, "Ball has been marvelously placed as a participant and observer of many extraordinary art situations." Indeed! Ginsberg's film maker friend Barbara Rubin was the catalyst to locating the property, and the mutual friend who brought a then rather aimless Gordon Ball on board to help with the prodigious efforts of realistically settling there. The details of getting this 100-year-old building into livable shape constitute at times a harrowing adventure. More than once, it seemed a Sisyphean task.

Ball brings a real insider perspective freed by the physical departure of most of the main players, which most importantly include Peter Orlovsky, Ray Bremser, Herbert Hunke, and Gregory Corso. The general reader at the very least will be moved to investigate the writings of this hip rogue's gallery.

Ginsberg's relationship with Orlovsky is a great document here unto itself, though it is clear that like an old married couple, they are now together for other reasons than sex. What those reasons are will probably take an entire volume by a future scholar to elucidate. The continual chaos of Orlovsky shooting speed on the premises paints a very different picture from the idyllic portrait Richard Avedon took of Ginsberg and Orlovsky hugging on the cover of *Evergreen Review* (August 1970), published in the middle of this tumultuous period. Ball's book gives Orlovsky's neutral expression in that photo a whole new patina. This revelation is not dissimilar to the wake-up call of finding out William Burroughs did not completely give up junk after his apomorphine cure. We may never know what Orlovsky's psychological problems were beyond his drug addiction, though his brother Julius, barely a sketch in both Ginsberg and Jack Kerouac's works, might today be diagnosed somewhere on the autism scale. Julius, never uttering a word in Kerouac's fiction, can at times be hilariously canny and surprisingly aware when he does speak – and Ball hears him speak a lot.

Orlovsky off speed is certainly lovable, as the title of his one volume of City Lights poetry, *Clean Asshole Poems & Smiling Vegetable Songs*, so wackily personifies. Lest one think that Orlovsky had no real chops, Ball quotes William Carlos Williams' description of Orlovsky as "the best lyric poet of his generation." Ball offers the following lines from Orlovsky as an example (the poem's title is not given): "I was born to remember a song about love – on a hill a butterfly / makes a cup that I drink from, walking over a bridge of / flowers" (48). Ball is also recording a time that would prove pivotal in Ginsberg's philosophical development. Though Ball correctly says that Ginsberg began his Buddhist studies prior to "Howl" (77), they were then purely intellectual and part of a sort of omnivorous gnosticism that would eventually include Hinduism and, to a lesser degree, the Sufi path. Kerouac took it much more seriously, as they famously debate in *The Dharma Bums*, with Ginsberg's Alvah Goldbrook being less than converted (Kerouac 28-29). Ginsberg would always prove interested, probably drawn by the humanist and complex philosophical elements, and calls himself a "Buddhist Jew" in Ball's book here (22), but the altar he builds in the attic incorporates just about every religion under the sun (75). In 1968, Ball recounts Ginsberg on William F. Buckley's TV interview program, *Firing Line,* repeating a Tibetan Buddhist exorcism mantra and then chanting the Hindu Hare Krishna mantra with his harmonium only a few minutes later. This mixture of non-theism and theism, of no fixed reference point (Buddha's *anatta*) and a soul, will be seriously challenged in a few short years under Tibetan lama Chogyam Trungpa's tutelage. The comforts and implications of a creator god and an eternal self will not survive in Ginsberg's metaphysics.

In 1969, Ginsberg began formal meditation practice an hour a day after tute-lage with Hindu master Swami Muktananda, in response to the increasingly violent language of leftist politics (371). Though not mentioned here, Ginsberg would meet Chogyam Trungpa Rinpoche by kismet, sharing a NYC cab in 1971, and the habit of sitting meditation would serve him well, though he would eventually switch from closed-eye silent mantra style to open-eyed attention to breath, which he found more grounding (Ginsberg 381). Ball does quote Ginsberg later in 1988, however: "My guru, Tibetan Lama Chogyam Trungpa, suggested I try a different one. . . 'Ah!' Which is appreciation of the spaciousness around us. Chanting Om so aggressively didn't intrigue people to enter that space, but probably just mystified them" (442).

Ball refers to Ginsberg's 1963 poem "The Change" as a rejection of Blakean visionary grasping for "Zen Buddhist ordinary mind set in everyday reality" (77). One can see "The Change" as some level of acceptance of being in a body, rather than "tripping out." Still, Ginsberg's proclamation of mutual tenderness and its fulfillment was his substitution for visions in 1963, not this "ordinary mind" solution of uncontrived "calm abiding" Trungpa later suggested to him. At one point, Ginsberg told Ball that he considered his most memorable line to be from "The Change": "so that I do / live I will die" (39). Spoken in 1968, one wonders if he would say the same towards the end of the near-30 years that remained in his life.

What really propelled him deeper into Buddhism's acceptance of suffering was the 1969 car accident in which he broke his hip. As Ball mentions, Ginsberg gave an *East Village Other* interview in which he rhetorically asked what happens if "you get carcrashes instead of cocksucks?" (442). At the time of his accident, Ginsberg wrote to Ferlinghetti, "I gotta get a new metaphysics. Body's too unreliable" (157). Likewise, he wrote to Charles Olson that "nausea hip to rib for a day and night realizing the body's a collapsable pain trap -& couldn't get past that. How'd I get into this body-stump?" (118).

Ball offers by example, again and again, that to really know Ginsberg was to love him. With the Ginsbergian taste of mortal sweetness and heartbreak, Ball finishes his memoir with Ginsberg's last word to Gregory Corso, which Corso repeated at his funeral:

Toodle-loo.

---Marc Olmsted

Works Cited

Ginsberg, Allen. *Spontaneous Mind: Selected Interviews, 1958-1996.* New York: Harper Collins, 2001.

Kerouac, Jack. *Dharma Bums.* New York: Signet, 1959.

The Cubalogues: Beat Writers in Revolutionary Havana.
Todd F. Tietchen (Gainesville, FL: University Press of Florida, 2010)

"... Now if in Korea we hear there
is continual killing, now if we rightly have no longer faith in our nations,
   now if we tire of futile decisions, we are at home among stranger
                                                                relations."
—Robert Duncan, "Writing at home in history"

For a brief two-year period following the 1959 revolution, the arts in Cuba were opened to new and daring currents that offered alternative ways of imagining the long and vexed relationship between that tiny Caribbean island and its northern neighbor. Likened by one of its participants to the Weimar era in Germany, this vibrant artistic renaissance coalesced around the Guillermo Cabrera Infante-edited literary journal *Lunes de Revolución* and was decidedly different in its revolutionary outlook than the "authorized" version of the Cuban Revolution its detractors sold to the American public. "We are not part of a group, neither literary nor artistic. . . ." announced *Lunes de Revolución*'s editors. "We do not have a definite political philosophy, although we do not reject certain systems which approach reality—and when we speak of systems, we are referring, for example, to dialectical materialism or psychoanalysis, or existentialism" (41-42). At the peak of its popularity, *Lunes de Revolución* had a circulation of 250,000 and championed the work of a new generation of revolutionary Cuban artists, writers, and film-makers, some of whom produced works—like *P.M.*, the 1960 Albert Maysles-influenced "free cinema" exploration of Havana nightlife directed by Infante's brother Sabá and Orlando Jiménez Leal—that soon ran afoul of the authorities.

But just as quickly as it had begun, this era of improvisation, experimentation and openness ended. On June 30, 1961, Fidel Castro announced in his address "A True Social Revolution Produces a Cultural Revolution (Words To The Intellectuals)" that henceforth "the most revolutionary artist will be that one who is prepared to sacrifice even his own artistic vocation for the Revolution" (*LANIC*). Cuban artistic and cultural life would from now on be subordinated to the ideological demands of national revolutionary policy. Shortly thereafter, *Lunes de Revolución* was shut down, its editor exiled, and by 1965 those engaged in the artistic underground had become "los infermos"—"the sick"—a dismissive term that reveals what little use the new revolutionary leadership had for art and literature that fell far outside the purview of orthodox revolutionary cultural praxis.

Todd Tietchen's *The Cubalogues: Beat Writers in Revolutionary Havana* is a densely argued study of those first-person narratives he terms "Cubalogues," a group of texts that constitute an "explicitly political subgenre of Beat travel narrative" (2). At the heart of the book are broadly contextualized readings of eyewitness Cubalogue accounts from the period 1960-61 by Lawrence Ferlinghetti ("Poet's Notes on Cuba"), Amiri Baraka ("Cuba Libre"), journalist Marc Schleifer ("Cuban Notebook"), and Harold Cruse ("A Negro Looks At Cuba"), along with a later Cubalogue-related prose piece by Allen Ginsberg ("Prose Contribution to Cuban Revolution"). Collectively, these narratives function for Tietchen as "acts of counter imagination" that challenge the parallels between the normative rhetoric of United States military and foreign policy and a public discursive sphere firmly under the sway of "long entrenched imperial tropes and the bifurcating rhetoric of Cold War politics" (155). Tietchen argues that these narratives imagine the relations between peoples, histories, politics, and art in ways that prefigure the culture and ethos of the New Left and its associated liberation movements.

If the Cubalogue is a form of "gone South" Beat travel narrative, it is one that unfolds within a decidedly more progressive political context than that traditionally afforded Latin American spaces in the U.S. literary imagination, long a series of libidinal contact zones for the Anglo Beat fantasies of figures such as William S. Burroughs and Jack Kerouac (9). By positioning his study firmly within the transnational and globalized approaches to Beat scholarship that have emerged in the last decade and that eschew the single-author literary-biographical model long familiar in the field[1], Tietchen effectively challenges our understandings of what constitutes Beat canonicity and why. He does so by enlarging the category "Beat" and by shifting his frame both spatially and historically, in the process successfully undermining the stereotype that Beat modes of subjectivity equate to an existential disengagement from collectively imagined political praxis. The five chapters at the heart of the book draw evidence from writers who have long been a part of the recognized Beat orbit (Baraka, Ferlinghetti and Ginsberg), while including others less obviously so (Cruse, Schleifer). Tietchen argues that all were shaped by their own direct, everyday experience of the Cuban revolution, an encounter that caused them fundamentally to reimagine their own relationship to art and revolutionary politics.

The book is organized around the metaphor of "stranger relations," which Tietchen draws from Robert Duncan's poem "writing at home in history." "Stranger relations" are mobilized throughout the study as a way of reimagining the relationship between the exclusionary and disciplinary modes of subjectivity demanded by the corporate liberal Cold War state—what Daniel Belgrad terms "the rationalization of mental attitude" (4)—and the alternative perspective of the excluded "stranger" who lurks at the margins of the national imaginary but who also shares affinities of outlook with other excluded groups. This relationship is imagined *across* national, cultural, and temporal boundaries in new networks that come to define a transnational oppositional culture that offers a broad and horizontally-configured alternative to a public sphere ordered by the "high seriousness" of Cold War pieties.

In his first chapter, for example, Tietchen explores poet Lawrence Ferlinghetti's involvement with issues of domestic censorship (a 1952 campaign against censorship, the "Howl" obscenity trial in 1956), anarcho-pacifism (his involvement with the Kenneth Rexroth circle), regional politics and aesthetics (his International Writer's Conference trip to Chile in 1959 with Ginsberg) and the forging of transnational rhetorical spaces (the 1956 City Lights publication of the Rexroth-translated *Thirty Spanish Poems of Love and Exile* containing poems by a selection of persecuted Spanish and Latin American writers) as evidence of Ferlinghetti's "stranger relations" within and across the local and regional spaces and histories of underground and countercultural politics. In this way, Tietchen not only recuperates Ferlinghetti from historian Van Gosse's charge that the poem "1000 Fearful Words for Fidel Castro" marks *the* pivotal moment of Ferlinghetti's political awakening, but also resituates and historicizes the broader question of Beat political engagement within a transnational perspective. Ferlinghetti, Tietchen argues, brought these progressive networks of relations to visibility a full decade before the New Left movements of the 1960s and 1970s reimagined them within a "Third World" context.

Similarly in his chapter on Amiri Baraka, Tietchen argues that Baraka's evolution from Beat fellow-traveler and civil-rights integrationist to an uncompromising advocate for the Black Arts Movement and Black Nationalism emerged directly from the experience of revolutionary forms of seeing and collective action that he captured in "Cuba Libre." The lived praxis of a revolutionary poetics that was also a *politically* engaged poetics pushed Baraka away from an earlier identification with existential modes of Beat disaffection, captured in his earlier work, such as the poem "Preface To A Twenty Volume Suicide Note," and towards the "stranger relations" of avant-garde forms such as jazz. Reimaging these forms post-Cuba, Baraka saw them as capable of "moving" oppressed peoples in the United States too, if framed with the same kind of revolutionary "attitude" or "stance" that had "moved" Cuba and her people during his visit. Thus, Baraka's story "The Screamers" firmly rejects a view of jazz that treats it as a vehicle for individual (and whitened) aesthetic awakenings. Instead, jazz offers Baraka a rhetorical space for an "ecstatic, completed" (80) and *collectivized* form of African-American cultural expression that stands in stark contrast to the repressive forms of self-denial embodied by the white jazz critic and the Black Church.

For Tietchen, then, "stranger relations" reconfigure connections made through political expression and belonging. They offer "a convergence of marginalized and differentiated human subjects across horizontal points of contact," throwing into sharp relief the limitations placed on political expectations by adherence to the so-called "reasonable" and "serious" (and hierarchically organized) modes of Cold War argumentation represented by figures such as Arthur Schlesinger Jr. and *The Partisan Review*'s Norman Podhoretz (14-15). As Baraka points out at the end of "Cuba Libre," far from offering a neutral political space, such modes are "always the historical manifestations of politically interested justifications" (73). In a compelling argument that echoes Daniel Belgrad's emphasis on the politically radical subjectivity promised by avant-garde forms of his "culture of spontaneity," Tietchen recasts stranger relations as *discursive* understandings. The bifurcated Cold War mindset shaping the U.S. public sphere led to a rhetorical blindness that foreclosed on the meaning of the Cuban Revolution ahead of time, rendering its networks of "strange relations" invisible and unutterable in the orthodox public sphere, a fact journalist Marc Schleifer discovered to his dismay: "What I'd stumbled upon was the problem of dealing with the faulty powers of American perception" (114). By broadening their understanding of liberation and possibility beyond the terms established by the Old Left's traditional labor-centered metaphysic, Tietchen argues that the Cubalogue writers were able to move past traditional loyalties and into positions that afforded a critical perspective on what became, after 1961, the increasingly authoritarian character of the Cuban Revolution. By 1965, for example, Che Guevara was calling for a form of revolutionary masculinity he labeled the "New Man" that opposed the decadent and cosmopolitan tendencies of "literary escapism and aesthetic avant-gardism" represented by organs such as *Lunes de Revolución.*

For Cubaloguer Marc Schleifer, this increasing inflexibility was evidence of reactionary sexual blind spots in the revolutionary imagination, lacunae highlighted by the plight of workers in the Cuban sex industry who faced inequity, poverty, and a Party leadership unconcerned with broader understandings of sexual freedom. For Allen Ginsberg, the Revolution's heteronormative turn evoked a characteristic response; to his Cuban hosts, he wondered aloud about Castro's childhood experiences with homosexuality, and said of Guevara, "I would very much like to go to bed with him" (121). Instead, of course, Ginsberg went on to become a spokesperson for the emerging counterculture and for what Tietchen terms the "Dostoyevskian strange": that "sense of personal genius and acceptance of all strangeness in people as their nobility." Ginsberg describes this as a "sort of Dostoyevskian-Shakespearean *know* [. . .] of things as mortal, tearful, transient, sacred"—a mode of awareness that, "realizing the relativity and limitation of all judgments and discriminations," challenges orthodox political classifications (136). By the mid-1960s, Ginsberg could criticize the Revolution for failing to live up to its early open promise of the "acceptance of all strangeness." By these gestures, too, he was expressing his own "strange relations" within emergent networks linking activist queer politics and his own personal poetic struggles against heteronormative domestic politics and foreign policy expressed in *Howl, and Other Poems.*

Then too, by 1965 Kerouac's retreat into a reified conservatism led him to condemn Ginsberg for his "pro-Castro bullshit and [. . .] long robe Messiah shot" (145). As I read Tietchen's account and the handful of intriguing references to Kerouac's take on Cuba, I wondered about the tensions *within* the Beat cohort over the meaning of the Revolution, and I was left wishing Tietchen had explored these tensions more fully. For instance, along which particular lines of identification did the Beats fracture over the Cuban question? How would a full accounting of these breaks change the ways we understand the wider category of "Beat" itself? And what happens to the term if we rethink it through Tietchen's "stranger relations," within broadly connected fields of affinities linking the socialism of the Old Left, the liberation movements of the New Left, and the crossing of regional and temporal boundaries? What of the relationship between the Cubalogues themselves and the much-vaunted Beat emphasis on open and spontaneous forms of representation? Other than a brief definitional discussion early in the book, Tietchen is generally silent on the formal qualities of these texts. Conceptually, "Beat" itself remains a largely unexplored term in this account, even though he widens the spatial and temporal axes of its use in a way that at times threatens to undo the presumed util-ity of the term as an analytic lens and also raises unanswered questions about the relationships between Beat literature and broader understandings of the American literary canon. This struck me as odd in a book otherwise so finely attuned to the political implications of our cultural and artistic representations.

Writing in 2003, critic Manuel L. Martinez argued that "[l]iterary historians (even the newer ones) and critics working on the reconstruction of American literary history characteristically know little in depth about the history, symbolo-gies, cultures, and discourses of the Americas." He calls for a literary perspective that refuses parochialism and the "limiting tacit assumptions" of single-author or mono-cultural points of view. He is admirably served in this regard by Tietchen's book. *The Cubalogues* is a valuable contribution to the emerging scholarship on transnational Beat identities and international Beat politics, a fascinating interven-tion in the "continuing project of a truly inclusive Americano studies" (Martinez 19).

---Phil Dickinson, *Bowling Green State University*

Notes

[1] See, for example, Ronna C. Johnson and Nancy M. Grace, *Girls Who Wore Black: Women Writing the Beat Generation.* New Brunswick, NJ: Rutgers UP, 2002; Timothy Gray, *Gary Snyder and the Pacific Rim: Creating Countercultural*

Community. Iowa City: U of Iowa P, 2006; Manuel Martinez, *Countering the Counterculture: Rereading Postwar American Dissent From Jack Kerouac to Tomás Rivera.* Madison: U of Wisconsin P, 2003; Kostas Myrsiades, ed. *The Beat Generation: Critical Essays.* New York: Peter Lang, 2002; Jennie Skerl, ed. *Reconstructing the Beats.* New York: Palgrave-Macmillan, 2004.

Works Cited

Belgrad, Daniel. *The Culture of Spontaneity: Improvisation and the Arts in Postwar America.* Chicago: U of Chicago P, 1998.

Castro, Fidel. "Speech to Intellectuals," June 30, 1961. LANIC: Latin American Network Information Center's Castro Speech Database http://lanic.utexas. edu/project/castro/db/1961/19610630.html November 20, 2010.

Duncan, Robert. *Writing, Writing.* Trask House, 1971.

Martinez, Manuel L. *Countering the Counterculture: Rereading Postwar Dissent from Jack Kerouac to Tomás Rivera.* Madison: U of Wisconsin P, 2003.

Capturing the Beat Moment: Cultural Politics and the Poetics of Presence.
Erik Mortensen (Carbondale, IL: Southern Illinois University Press, 2011)

"Being as Now has been reinvented,
I have devised a new now
Entering the real Now
At last
Which is now."
   —Allen Ginsberg, "Bad Poem"

According to thirteenth-century Japanese Zen Master Dōgen Zenji, founder of the Sōtō lineage of Zen Buddhism, there are 6,400,099,180 moments in a single day. Each of these moments presents us with an opportunity to realize the fleeting impermanence of time's true nature and to practice what Indian Buddhist philosopher-patriarch Nāgārjuna calls the "flux of arising and decaying" (Katagiri 3). Since the late 1950s, Buddhism's discourse of radical presentism has become a commonplace in the West, manifesting itself in a bewildering array of syncretic practices that cohere around the ritualized and repetitive act of returning to "the fact that we find ourselves, always, in a certain time, in a certain body, living a certain kind of life" (Cook 53). Increasingly too, postwar Anglo-American critical theory has turned to the terrain of the everyday, a realm at once familiar, mundane and so transparently obvious as to be scarcely worthy of comment and yet which, paradoxically, appears largely invisible to the analytic tools of orthodox academic disciplines such as sociology and ethnography.[1] Although the traditions of "everyday life studies" and Buddhism bring very different modalities to bear on this quotidian ground, both have emerged as powerful counter-narratives to the spectacle of global capital's ever more intimate colonization of the spaces and moments of our daily lives.

All of which serves, I hope, as a useful introduction to the central premise of Erik Mortensen's *Capturing the Beat Moment: Cultural Politics and the Poetics of Presence*, a theoretically savvy if often unsatisfying study of the multiple and ambiguous relationships between Beat writers and their articulations of an "evanescent present" (1). For Mortensen, the Beat project of capturing the moment occupies a liminal middle ground between the modernist conceits of a subject grounded by embodied experience (yet always trending towards fantasies of utopian totality), and the claims of a postmodern subject teetering on the brink of a decentered and dispersed incoherence. In this view, the Beats are "early-postmodernists," riding "the cusp of the modern- postmodern split." They stake out a both/and positionality that incorporates modernist conceptions of language derived from corporeality *and* the postmodern desire to transcend that corporeality in favor of new and experimental configurations of experience (8).

Contemporary scholarship on the Beats, Mortensen reminds us, tends to fall into one of three broad categories; the single author study, the broader thematic treatment such as Michael Davidson's *The San Francisco Renaissance*, and the cross-disciplinary inquiry exemplified by studies such as Daniel Belgrad's *The Culture of Spontaneity*. Mortensen includes *Capturing the Beat Moment* within the second of these traditions, suggesting that it provides significant payoffs. One of these payoffs is that we get to understand "how a concept, current in the culture at large, gets reworked by a specific group with specific interests" (9). He asserts that his critical engagement with an expanded Beat canon represents a break from previous Beat scholarship, and boldly suggests that this approach not only promises to "yield a better understanding of the Beat moment and its place in postwar literary and cultural history but will likewise allow for a more fruitful conception of how Beat thinking on the moment might be utilized for everyday lived existence" (10).

Each of Mortensen's five chapters revolves around representative thematic examples that are carefully framed within terms he establishes in his introduction. Beat writers exemplify an early-postmodern subjectivity in action and they share both the modernist predilection for totalizing grand narratives and the postmodern concern with subject-less undecidability and relativism. Mortensen's liminal Beat subject, tacking back and forth across the edge of early-postmodern cultural modalities, is a vividly rendered organizing figure and is deployed as such in all of his chapters and across the full range of his examples. Whether attempting to escape the "readymade schemes" of the postwar corporate-liberal organization of time and space (chapter 1), forging ways to mobilize the epiphanal moment as a visionary repertoire to be used in the future (chapter 2), using orgasm to return to and also transcend the body (chapter 3), exploiting the gap between photographic representations and their textual supplements to enact memory (chapter 4), or anticipating the heterotopic social practices of 1960s countercultural groups (chapter 5), this subject relentlessly reimagines "how to stay open to the new without settling into one particular outlook or becoming enmeshed in the desire for continual novelty" (57).

Take the trope of orgasm for example, which Mortensen explores in the third chapter, "Immanence and Transcendence: Reich, Orgasm and the Body." Both the early-postmodern Beat emphasis on embodiment—the "body is the site of modernist wholeness and totality par excellence," after all—and the desire to transcend the body via a "belief in openness and multiplicity that is a hallmark of the postmodern" are manifested through a moment of orgasm that simultaneously essentializes and relativizes the body (86). Ejaculation and conception are grounded by modernist frameworks such as myth; here Mortensen suggests that William Carlos Williams' *Kora In Hell: Improvisations* privileges the role of the author-hero and Kora's own role as bringer of life, a reading he supports with Stuart Davis' cover art of sperm and egg used for the 1920 edition of the book. Williams and Davis represent a modernist agenda that turns "artistic production into a singular act of will that is nevertheless reproduced across moments of history" (89). The postmodern orgasm transcends the gross materiality of the body, relativizing it as an ungrounded and fragmentary figure. For Mortensen, Andres Serrano's 1989 photograph "Untitled VII (Ejaculate in Trajectory)" is the paradigmatic decontextualized postmodern body, literally and metaphorically floating free of the anchoring certainties of earlier modernist generative myth, now a figure of difference rather than of essentialism. Characteristically, Beat depictions of orgasm assume both figural qualities at once. The cover of Gregory Corso's 1959 poetry collection *Long Live Man* features a photograph of the Crab Nebula that ambiguously conflates both "sperm and firmament" and is "characteristic of Corso's desire to elevate the moment of orgasm to cosmic significance" (91). Likewise, Corso's first poem "Man" not only essentializes masculinity in terms of biological heritage but grants man the power to overcome biology through the "magic wand" of a penis "that drives the species forward in a never-ending process of building, unbuilding, rebuilding that knows no teleological end" (91). Thus Beat writing on orgasm reveals the influence of both a Reichian insistence on orgasm as the essential recuperative act of return to an authentic body *and* adds orgasm to the repertoire of practices mobilized by the Deleuzian Body without Organs. Orgasm becomes, in this reading, "the most essential act a human male can perform and the most transcendent" (92).

Mortensen casts an impressively wide net in *Capturing the Beat Moment*. He offers the usual lengthy treatments of the traditional Beat triumvirate of Kerouac, Ginsberg, and Burroughs along with a largely familiar supporting cast of "other" Beats (Corso, Baraka, di Prima, Jones, Johnson, Vega, Kandel, etc.). But it is his willingness to engage with a diverse swath of ideas and examples drawn from critical theorists and philosophers as varied as Heidegger, Lukacs, Merleau-Ponty, Deleuze and Guattari, Benjamin, Jameson, Lyotard, and Barthes that can best be read as evidence for the emerging critical legitimacy of recent Beat scholarship and its alignment with the discourses of academic theory.

At times, however, this eclecticism muddies rather than clarifies Mortensen's theoretical waters and lends a haphazard quality to his argument. For example, he periodizes the Beat moment as "early-postmodern" but never consistently addresses the important questions this maneuver raises. What of the relationship between early-postmodern Beat writing and the genealogies of modernism itself? As Marjorie Perloff suggests, here at the dawn of the twenty-first century, "it is the variety of modernisms that strikes us; indeed, the totalization often attributed to modernism belongs much less to the literature of modernism than to its theorists" (qtd. in Wallace 3). Perhaps Mortensen's acknowledgement of these wider debates, or at the very least an explicit concession that his usage of the modern/postmodern rubric admits something of what Rob Wallace terms "strategic essentialism" might have added a useful caveat to some of his broader claims (3). What too of the possibility, raised by postmodern thinkers such as David Harvey, Zygmunt Bauman, and others, that the presentism of the early-postmodern can be tied to the emergence in the West of a particular *form* of postwar consumer capitalism?[2] Curiously given Mortensen's arguments elsewhere in the book, he never really explores this context, although tantalizingly he does skirt it on occasion, suggesting that the Beat affinity for Zen Buddhism in this period stems primarily from Zen's resistance to institutionalization, its emphasis on the experiential, and its resonance with antimaterialism (74). A passing reference to Belgrad's linkage of Zen and spontaneity merely suggests that Mortensen has missed a wider opportunity to tie the Beat poetics of presence to a thorough contextual frame that understands the connections between aesthetic forms and the social and economic formations of which they are a part. In the final analysis then, his use of the rubric of modern and postmodern remains under-theorized, which is an important drawback for a study as ambitious as this.

Despite these caveats, I found much to like about *Capturing the Beat Moment*. In particular, the emphasis Mortensen places on spatial and temporal issues in Beat writing is refreshing and duly expands the range of theoretical registers now brought to bear in the field. These raise vitally important new directions for Beat scholarship: a couple of obvious questions present themselves. Given the oft remarked-upon qualities of orality and performativity in Beat writing, how might we understand the relationship between Mortensen's poetics of presence and practices such as improvisation? And if the Beats do "desire to live and write the present as it continually unfolds through space and time," then what does it mean to talk of "the present" in this way, and what does "living" and "writing" this present moment feel and look like (1)? In beginning to sketch out speculative lines of inquiry such as these, Mortensen treads a characteristically ambiguous line; a poetics of presence is a poetics that regards moments as both ordinary and yet filled too with immanent, perhaps even transcendent, possibility "for a new trajectory into the void, a chance to change the direction of one's life" (83). As an example of this, he cites women Beat writers such as Diane di Prima and Hettie Jones and their negotiation of the highly gendered space of 1950s domesticity, hinting in the process at a positively de Certeauvian understanding of everyday life riddled with the complex, heterogeneous traces and inscriptions of social and economic histories that are intimately tied to the ordinary experience and practices of bodies, acting and being acted upon (34-41).

"Everyday life invites a kind of theorizing that throws our most cherished *theoretical* values and practices into crisis," writes critic Ben Highmore in his introduction to *The Everyday Life Reader.* Can theory be "found [in] the pages of a novel, in a suggestive passage of description in an autobiography, or in the street games of children? What if theory (the kind that is designated as such) was beneficial for attending to the everyday, not via its systematic interrogations, but through its poetics, its ability to render the familiar strange?" (3). For me, the final value of Mortensen's book lies precisely in the possibilities it raises for this kind of rethinking of the relationship among Beat writing, the lived terrain of the everyday, and a poetics that performs a form of attention to the moment-by-moment flux of daily life. If, as Mortensen puts it, the "current social situation is in many ways merely an intensification of the beliefs and constructs developed in the postwar era that serve to cut everyone off from truly experiencing the world," then perhaps a renewed commitment to a Beat poetics of presence can make intelligible our own estranged, inauthentic, and ever-mutable historical moment (16)?

---Phil Dickinson, *Bowling Green State University*

Notes

¹ See, for example, Michael E. Gardiner, *Critiques of Everyday Life* (London: Routledge, 2000); Stephen Johnstone, *The Everyday: Documents of Contemporary Art* (London: Whitechapel, 2008); Ben Highmore, *Everyday Life and Cultural Theory: An Introduction* (London: Routledge, 2002); Ben Highmore, ed. *The Everyday Life Reader* (London: Routledge, 2002); Michael Sheringham, *Everyday Life: Theories and Practices from Surrealism to the Present* (Oxford: Oxford UP, 2006).

² See Bertens, chapter 10 for a useful overview of these debates.

Works Cited

Belgrad, Daniel. *The Culture of Spontaneity: Improvisation and the Arts in Postwar America*. Chicago: U. of Chicago P., 1998.

Bertens, Hans. *The Idea of the Postmodern: A History*. London: Routledge, 1995.

Cook, Francis Dojun. *How To Raise An Ox: Zen Practice as Taught in Master Dōgen's Shōbōgenzō*. Boston: Wisdom, 2002.

Davidson, Michael. *The San Francisco Renaissance: Poetics and Community at Mid- Century*. Cambridge: Cambridge UP, 1989.

Highmore, Ben, ed. *The Everyday Life Reader*. London: Routledge, 2002

---. *Michel de Certeau: Analysing Culture*. New York: Continuum, 2006.

Katagiri, Dainin. *Each Moment Is the Universe: Zen and the Way of Being Time*. Boston: Shambhala, 2008.

Wallace, Rob. *Improvisation and the Making of American Literary Modernism*. New York: Continuum, 2010.

Queer (25th Anniversary Edition).
William S. Burroughs, Edited with an introduction by Oliver Harris (New York, NY: Penguin, 2010)

In 2010, Penguin Books published a new edition of William Burroughs' *Queer*. Edited by Oliver Harris, the 2010 edition commemorates the 25th anniversary of *Queer*'s initial publication. Part trade paperback and part critical edition, the 2010 edition is a hybrid text of sorts. *Queer*[1] is not only readable and saleable, but also the most scholarly treatment of the novel to date. *Queer* is comprised of an editor's introduction, a clear text, an appendix, and endnotes. The clear text can function independently or in concert with the paratextual elements of *Queer*, depending on the proclivities of the reader. With the exception of approximately one hundred emendations where he preferred the original manuscript, Harris accepted the majority of the decisions made by the editor of the 1985 edition, James Grauerholz. Harris details many of his emendations that differ from the 1985 edition in the section titled "endnotes." *Queer*'s endnotes operate similarly to an editorial apparatus. The endnotes do not include a list of each editorial intervention, but they do provide a dense and well-researched wrangling of *Queer*'s manuscript history.

The most significant difference between *Queer* and the 1985 edition is structural: that is, the decision to begin *Queer* with his thirty-six page editor's introduction and move Burroughs' introduction from the 1985 edition to the appendix marks Harris' most influential action. Harris' introduction effectively preempts what Burroughs has to say in his introduction to the 1985 edition. Devaluing the more scandalous elements of Burroughs' introduction, Harris shifts the focus to *Queer*'s compositional context and clarifies how it relates to Burroughs' development as a writer. *Queer*, Burroughs' second novel, was written after *Junky* and before *Yage Letters*. Burroughs had planned to write *Queer* using the same "factualist" narrative technique he used to produce *Junky*. However, in the course of writing *Queer*, Burroughs developed a complement to the flat, realist narrative mode of *Junky*. The complement, termed a "routine" by Burroughs, occurs in *Queer* during moments when the factualist narrative dissolves into a stream of surrealist phrases and images, each attempting to astonish more than the last. Harris links the dissolution of the realist narrative in *Queer* with the origin of *Naked Lunch* stating, "You might say that in its very failure to sustain a straight narrative method *Queer* became itself, and described like this, we can also begin to see how its failures predicted Burroughs' greatest success...the chaotic mosaic of *Naked Lunch*" (xvii).

Harris presents alternative sources of inspiration for *Queer* that contrast with those Burroughs detailed in his introduction to the 1985 edition. One source Harris connects with the composition of *Queer* and Burroughs' development as a writer is Jack Kerouac. While writing *Queer* in 1952, Burroughs shared an apartment with Kerouac in Mexico City. When Kerouac arrived in Mexico City, he brought examples of, and an enthusiasm for, his recently developed narrative technique of spontaneous prose. Living with Kerouac and reading parts of his unpublished novels *Visions of Cody* and *Dr. Sax*, Burroughs was likely influenced by the performative nature, associative logic, and wordplay of spontaneous prose. Harris writes, "It's possible that Kerouac's passion for experimenting with form in *Cody* and *Sax* has an influence on *Queer*. In the very least, it might have led Burroughs to worry less about the unstable roughness of his own new manuscript" (xix). Kerouac's *Spontaneous Prose* passages and Burroughs' routines both exhibit associative logic, wordplay, and tempos that frequently build toward a climactic verbal release. The relationship between Burroughs and Kerouac during their time in Mexico City was symbiotic. Burroughs and his then unpublished novel *Queer* had an impact on Kerouac as well. Harris notes that Kerouac's *Dr. Sax* "reveals multiple traces—in theme, allusion, and specific phrasings—of his readings of Burroughs' manuscript" of *Queer* (xix).

The epistolary form is the second source that Harris links with Burroughs' development as a writer and experimentation with narrative in *Queer*. During the time Burroughs was writing *Queer*, he frequently penned letters to Adelbert Lewis Marker, upon whom the *Queer* character Allerton is based. Marker was Burroughs' former lover and the object of his unrequited affection by the summer of 1952. Describing the impact of Burroughs' wanton letters to Marker on the composition of *Queer*, Harris writes "his trademark form and virtuoso style were driven by his desire-fueled letters" (xxxii). Although none of the letters Burroughs sent to Marker during the composition of *Queer* are extant, Harris suggests that the form and content of the letters likely parallel the routines Lee spoke to Allerton in *Queer*.

In his introduction to the 1985 edition, Burroughs emphasizes the effects of heroin withdrawal and the death of his wife Joan Vollmer on the composition of *Queer*. Relating heroin withdrawal to the routines spoken by Lee, *Queer*'s narrator, Burroughs writes, "While the addict is indifferent to the impression he creates in others, during withdrawal he may feel the compulsive need for an audience, and this is clearly what Lee seeks in Allerton [. . .] So he invents a frantic attention-getting format which he calls the Routine" (129). Burroughs' assertion is admittedly confusing. He fails to differentiate between himself and the narrator Lee, but what is very clear is that Burroughs conflates the development of the routine with the symptoms of heroin withdrawal. Burroughs goes on to state that the death of his wife Joan had an even greater effect on *Queer* and his development as a writer. Burroughs writes "the book is motivated and formed by an event which is never mentioned, in fact is carefully avoided: the accidental shooting death of my wife, Joan, in September 1951" (131). Burroughs continues, "I am forced to the appalling conclusion that I would have never become a writer but for Joan's death, and to a realization of the extent to which this event has motivated and formulated my writing" (135). Burroughs' description of the influence of Joan's death on *Queer* is one of the major reasons Harris relegated the 1985 introduction to the appendix. Harris bemoans Burroughs' mention of Joan's death, stating that those lines "are quoted as often as anything he ever wrote" (xi), going on to state Burroughs' "revelation also had the perverse effect of framing the text with such a sensational context that it all but obscured both the fiction itself and any other reality behind it" (xii).

Reframing the text of *Queer* and mitigating the sensational aspects of Burroughs' introduction is part of Harris' larger goal to present Burroughs as a serious and important author who deserves critical attention. With his rigorous editing and considered re-packaging of *Junky*, *Queer*, and *Yage Letters*, Harris has established the texts that will be significant to the study of Burroughs for years to come. Harris' intervention is indicative of a shift in the power dynamics between Beat Generation writers and their critics. Representative of this shift is the relegation of Burroughs' introduction to the appendix and the absence of a single blurb from a fellow Beat Generation writer. While the 1985 edition of *Queer* contained a blurb from Allen Ginsberg, the 25th Anniversary edition displays a single blurb from the Los Angeles *Times*.

From a critical standpoint, *Queer* is an improvement of the 1985 edition. Penguin Books, conscious of the unfolding reputation of Beat Generation authors and the growing classroom appeal for its Beat Generation backlist, appears to be moving towards editions that are more critically viable. Hybrid texts such as *Queer* maintain the marketability of trade paperbacks with the increased academic rigor that will ensure the long-term viability of Beat Generation authors.

---Ryan Ehmke, *Naval Academy Preparatory School*

Notes

[1] In subsequent references, I refer to the 2010 edition as simply *Queer*. For the remainder of the essay I refer to the initial publication of *Queer* as "the 1985 edition."

Jack Kerouac and Allen Ginsberg: The Letters.
Edited by Bill Morgan and David Stanford
(New York, NY: Viking Penguin, 2010.)

Their correspondence lasted two decades, carried across continents, and endured deaths and divorces, wars and revolutions. But it got off to a shaky start. In his fourth letter to Allen Ginsberg, on September 6, 1945, Jack Kerouac took his new friend to task for not revealing more of himself. "I honestly wish that you had more essential character," he wrote. "But then, perhaps you have that and are afraid to show it" (25). Kerouac was right on target; he read Ginsberg's character and personality immediately. Ginsberg wrote back soon afterward, but it took him a long time before he addressed the issues that Kerouac raised. Throughout most of the letter, he talked about their mutual friends, such as William S. Burroughs, and his own reading in Rimbaud. Only at the very end did he stand up for himself and accuse Kerouac of being "condescending to [me]" (27). He added in a P.S. that "I'd like to save your letters."

Of course, he did save them, much as Kerouac saved Ginsberg's letters to him. Without their instinct to archive their correspondence this book of nearly 200 letters from 1944 to 1963 would not exist. In many of the letters, Kerouac tries to draw out Ginsberg and to persuade him to be more authentic and more candid than he was. Indeed, Kerouac is more consistently open about himself than Ginsberg is open about himself. Again and again, Kerouac reveals the deepest parts of himself, as in an April 1948 letter in which he writes, "It's terrible never to find a father in a world chock full of fathers of all sorts. Finally you find yourself as father, but then you never find a son to father" (33). Reading letters such as this one helps one to understand why Kerouac wanted to make *On the Road* a novel about the main character's search for his father. In addition to the archetypical theme of the son's search for the father, there was an intensely personal element.

Bill Morgan and David Stanford, the two editors of this hefty volume, sorted through about three hundred letters before fixing on the published subset. They have written a very short introduction and the briefest of notes to some of the letters. That seems to be wise. A reader does not have to wade through a long critical essay about Kerouac, Ginsberg, and the Beats, and can instead go almost directly to the letters themselves. About a third have already been published in the masterful two-volume collection of Kerouac's letters that Ann Charters edited. Scholars have had access to these letters in libraries for decades, and students and teachers who are familiar with the biographies of both Kerouac and Ginsberg will recognize many passages from them. So, *The Letters* is not as startling as it might have been, but it is an essential book for anyone and everyone who wants to understand the relationship between these two men who were at the heart of the Beat Generation.

Almost everyone who played a part in Ginsberg's and Kerouac's lives shows up in the letters, and so they provide a kind of group portrait. David Kammerer, Lucien Carr, Joan Adams, Hal Chase, and, of course, William S. Burroughs make appearances in the earliest letters. Before long, they are also comparing notes about Neal Cassady. In fact, Kerouac explains in a letter to Ginsberg on May 18, 1948, that he has written a letter of recommendation for Cassady, who had applied for a job as a brakeman on the Southern Pacific railroad.

Reading these letters makes one appreciate how little time these men actually spent together in the same places, and how long they stayed connected by writing to one another across great distances. Sometimes their letters are emotionally raw, as when Kerouac writes to Ginsberg on January 21, 1958, to say, "Don't forget I love you, but I'm afraid of you now, and for you" (390). One feels the depth of their emotional ties, and especially Ginsberg's neediness. In the last letter in this book, from October 6, 1963, he asks Kerouac, "Will you love me ever?" (475).

For my money, this is the best single resource book about the Kerouac-Ginsberg connection. It takes one inside the tangled knot of their relationship, and it shows the people who gathered around them, their family members, friends, and lovers. *The Letters* will aid any scholar of the Beats. It will also touch the hearts of everyone who has ever read *On the Road* and *Howl* and who has been moved by those two classics. *The Letters* is a big book – more than 500 pages – and after reading it, one might well feel as though one has lived side-by-side with Kerouac and Ginsberg, coming to know them as authors and as friends.

---Jonah Raskin, *Sonoma State University*

Modern American Counter Writing: Beats, Outriders, Ethnics.
A. Robert Lee (Routledge, 2010)

Modern American Counter Writing: Beats, Outriders, Ethnics by A. Robert Lee is an impressive product of many years of scholarship on post-World War II dissident American literature. The book consists of sixteen essays: nine written for this volume, seven previously published but substantially revised, and one reprint. Organized into three parts according to the categories in the subtitle, the essays are a mix of broad surveys and those that focus on one or a few writers, with four chapters on Beat writers, nine chapters on ethnic literature, and three chapters on three writers designated as outriders. Each essay stands alone as a thorough introduction to its subject, beginning with the foundation of historical/biographical and critical background, identifying conflicting assessments or frequently debated issues, then proceeding to Lee's original analysis of specific works. The footnotes for each chapter provide comprehensive critical bibliographies. Thus, the book is a valuable resource for readers who may be interested in a particular author or authors or in the discursive formations of canon or anti-canon in which they are placed.

Lee's discussion of a diverse collection of writers is theorized through the portmanteau term of "counter writing," which is defined in a preliminary fashion in the introduction and further developed and complicated throughout the book. Counter writing includes the dissidents, contrarians, bad boys/bad girls/bad subjects who produce counter-texts to America's assumed consensual order or "managed consensus." They are not a unified tradition or group, but a constant presence in

American literary history of writers against the grain. Lee's book, however, is testimony to the prominence of counter writers in the second half of the twentieth century, destabilizing not only canon formation in the traditional sense, but also standard literary pigeonholes such as "Beat" or "ethnic." This questioning of labels and canons is one of the book's larger themes. The particularity of Lee's style—avoiding overarching generalizations and defining counter writing through specific analysis of individual texts and suggestive metaphors—encourages the reader to construct her own definitions and to make connections between writers not always seen in relation to each other.

In the four chapters on Beat writers in Part I, Lee works within an expanded definition of Beat that includes women, African-Americans, and writers outside the United States. The first essay is a comprehensive overview of the Beat movement that problematizes the canon. He identifies what has become the assumed or de facto canon of Allen Ginsberg, Jack Kerouac, Gregory Corso, William S. Burroughs, and Lawrence Ferlinghetti, based on their first publications from 1955 to 1962 that brought public recognition to the Beats as a movement and installed these authors as the leaders or icons, but at the same time relegating numerous Beat-related authors to a "shadow canon." By focusing on explication of texts, rather than authors, Lee expands the canon to include John Clellon Holmes, LeRoi Jones, Carl Solomon, Michael McClure, Diane di Prima, Robert Rosenthal, Bonnie Bremser/Frazer, Harold Norse, Herbert Huncke, and Joyce Johnson. Fifteen writers receive original critical analysis of their work. As the reader proceeds through this introductory essay, she participates in exploring a sense of Beat as (in Lee's words) a literary efflorescence, a circuit of texts, an orbit, a diverse archive of voice, an inclusive gallery, a pathway, a web, a register, a signature, a plurality of expressive ways operating across texts, a linkage of life views, and an open idiom. Ultimately, one is persuaded that Beat is a more complex and wider body of constituent authorship than a few of the more famous participants; nor are Beats confined to a particular decade. Most important is a rejection of fixed icons and definitions in favor of an array of Beat-inflected specific works that oscillate and affiliate within a web of plural voices. The initial "opening of the canon" is followed by an essay devoted to three Beat women poets (di Prima, Joanne Kyger, and Anne Waldman) which also includes an overview of women's participation in Beat writing, an essay on Ted Joans' body of work, and an essay on "Beat International." This last essay bookends the first, beginning with a survey of Beat international geography, then focusing on three writers: Michael Horovitz (British), Andrei Voznesensky (Russian), and Kazuko Shiraishi (Japanese). In this essay, Beat is configured as live counter voice, Beat-linked voicing, a trace, an affiliation, counter-note, transcultural affinity, an international ripple-effect, a thread of the 1960s counter-culture, and finally a transcultural circuit/counter-circuit (the latter an example of oscillation rather than definition). Within such a configuration of Beat, Voznesensky, a Soviet Union poet of the 1960s, can be accepted as Beat-affiliated.

The nine chapters in Part III on American ethnic writers, impressive in its breadth and depth, display Lee's erudition in this field. (Indeed, he has published five previous books on multicultural American literature.) The first essay, aptly entitled "ethnics behaving badly," is a survey of black, native, Latino/a and Asian-American texts selected for their "contrarian verve." Nine authors are discussed in some detail (Ishmael Reed, Darryl Pinckney, Gerald Vizenor, Leslie Marmon Silko, Oscar Zeta Acosta, Richard Rodriquez, Monica Stone, Max Yeh), and many others are mentioned. The chapter begins with Zora Neale Hurston as an earlier exemplar of the refusal of victimhood, anticipating later writers who complicate, outmaneuver, and subvert stereotypic expectations about belonging to an assumed minority niche. The other touchstone author in this chapter and for this entire section of the book is Gerald Vizenor, whose work regularly challenges social, literary, and linguistic stereotypes and who is known for his neologisms, such as "postindian" and "survivance." The next chapter is a broad survey of U.S. poetry of immigrancy and migrancy, referencing dozens of poets (including Euro-Americans) who reflect this perennial American experience. Three more focused survey chapters are devoted to multicultural Hispanic-American literature of the 1990s, Chinese-American poetry, and Japanese-American literature. The final four chapters each treat one writer: Frank Chin, Jessica Hagendorn, William Demby, and Gerald Vizenor. Part III is a detailed mapping of "ethnic" literature after World War II, which questions the label through counter-texts that establish their authors as American artists against the grain, especially those who write postmodern fiction.

The section on "outriders" (Part II) consists of three chapters, one each devoted to Hunter Thompson, Joan Didion, and Kathy Acker. Again, Lee provides an excellent comprehensive essay on each writer. However, the designation of "outrider" is not presented with the detail provided for "Beat" or "ethnic," so that the selection and placement of these authors in a separate category is not convincing. Thompson and Acker could easily have been discussed within the penumbra of Beat, especially since each has acknowledged the influence of Beat writers, and their textual homage to Kerouac and Burroughs, respectively, is prominent in their work. Classifying Didion as an outsider/outrider is questionable, since, as Lee himself mentions, she writes from a conservative, even elitist, stance and has had an establishment, or insider, career from the beginning. In this case, Lee's concrete, inductive method does not succeed in establishing a persuasive classification, although certainly the individual essays are valuable— each a thorough comprehensive analysis of the writer's career.

Modern American Counter Writing is the work of a mature scholar whose essays reflect years of research and teaching; it builds on prior research, but is wholly original in its analysis and interpretation of texts, as well as its theoretically sophisticated approach to literary history and canon formation. Apropos of a recent discussion on the Beat Studies Association listserv, this book shows how good scholarship is done. Lee is also a good read: he wears his learning lightly and writes in an engaging style that promotes interest in the writers under discussion, especially those that may be new to the reader.

---Jennie Skerl, retired, *West Chester University*

Lawrence Ferlinghetti, 60 Anni di Pittura (60 Years of Painting). Edited by Giada Diano and Elisa Polimeni (Silvana Editoriale, 2010)

The enduring success of *Howl and Other Poems* and *A Coney Island of the Mind* perhaps overshadows Lawrence Ferlinghetti's fame as a prolific painter. During a career of more than sixty years, Ferlinghetti has produced more than 2000 works of visual art, including paintings, assemblages, silk screens, lithographs, and drawings. In 2010 in Italy, in both Rome (26 February-25 April) and Reggio Calabria (5 May-1 July), an exhibition of fifty-four paintings by Ferlinghetti revealed his career as a visual artist. Now Silvana Editoriale has published *60 Years of Painting*, an oversized collection of representative works from the exhibitions in Italy. The volume also includes tributes from the mayors of the cities that hosted the exhibitions, critical essays on Ferlinghetti's achievements, selected writings by Ferlinghetti, and several appendices to provide biographical and bibliographical data. Texts appear in both Italian and English; a sequence of large black-and-white photographs includes several portraits of Ferlinghetti and scenes from his studio and his cabin in Big Sur.

60 Years of Painting is not the first and only oversized collection of works of visual art by Ferlinghetti. In 1997, after an exhibition in Rome at the Palazzo delle Esposizione (7 March-30 June 1996), Progetti Museali Editore published *Ferlinghetti: The Poet as Painter*, a volume of interpretive and critical writings with photographs from the Beat era and selected paintings from the era 1959-1996. In 2003 City Lights published *Life Studies Life Stories*, a collection of eighty works on paper. This volume focuses on drawings and includes few words and no photos. In 2005 Zero Gravità published *Lawrence Ferlinghetti: Creazione del Verbo Fluxare*, a catalog of thirty-three silk screens on cloth. This catalog reveals Ferlinghetti's unique position with respect to the artistic movement known as

Fluxus and his extensive incorporation of language in silk screens demonstrating his coining of the verb *fluxare.*

60 Years of Painting, while not displacing other collections of paintings, drawings, and prints by Ferlinghetti, certainly is the most complete and up-to-date collection of Ferlinghetti's work as a visual artist. The chronological arrangement of the works contributes to the viewer's appreciation of Ferlinghetti's artistic development. *Deux* (1950), which is Lawrence Ferlinghetti's first painting, is oil on canvas in black and white. Smooth, clear strokes define the faces of blindfolded lovers who seem to revolve in anticipation of intimacy. *The Birds* (1958), like many other works by Ferlinghetti, betrays the artist's limitations in drawing, but the distribution of color on the canvas corresponds to similar properties in more abstract works, such as *Manhattan Transit* (1959) and *Night #2* (1959).

The allusive characteristics of Ferlinghetti's paintings are evident in *The Death of Neal Cassady at San Miguel de Allende* (1982-1998), in which Ferlinghetti incorporates the phrase "cocksman and Adonis" from Ginsberg's "Howl." In *Bird Arising (After Morris Graves)* (1991), Ferlinghetti insists that the viewer see Ferlinghetti's bird as a reflection on similar images in the works of Morris Graves. In *Spanish Landscape* (1991), Ferlinghetti prompts the viewer to recall Goya's *The Third of May, 1808: The Execution of the Defenders of Madrid* (1814), but Ferlinghetti's image is far less representational than Goya's. In *Pablo* (1992), Ferlinghetti surrounds Picasso with Cubist images that spring from his imagination, making Ferlinghetti's painting a comment on Picasso's place in the history of art. Other works in *60 Years of Painting* call attention to Proust, Pound, Freud, Tennyson, Beckett, and the New York School.

While some social protest is expressed in works such as *Liberty on Earth* (1992), *The Upper Classes* (1992), and *This Is Not a Man* (1993-1994), most of the images in *60 Years of Painting* reveal personal emotion and engagement with famous artists. This reduced emphasis on social justice is difficult to correlate with Ferlinghetti's current writing, especially *Poetry as Insurgent Art* (New Directions, 2007), which expresses the view that art and activism are inseparable.

Also reduced in the selection of paintings in *60 Years of Painting* is the combination of image and text. In numerous paintings Ferlinghetti includes writing almost as if he were placing graffiti on his own canvases. While works such as *Ezra Pound* (2009) and *This Is Not a Man* (1993-1994) include text, the works included in *Ferlinghetti: The Poet as Painter* and *Lawrence Ferlinghetti: Creazione del Verbo Fluxare* reveal Ferlinghetti's combination of image and text more frequently and more profoundly.

Among the critical essays included in *60 Years of Painting* is "Lawrence Ferlinghetti and the Culture in Action" by Maria Anita Stefanelli, who remarks, "In his sixty years of work with brush and colors, Ferlinghetti mentally crosses many artistic paths without losing sight of the political and social value of reality" (35). Stefanelli refers to *Pictures of the Gone World*, *A Coney Island of the Mind*, and *Poetry as Insurgent Art*, drawing connections with Ferlinghetti's paintings, including *Winged Victory* (1992), *Birds Leaving Earth* (1998), and *Liberty on Earth*.

To *60 Years of Painting* Susan and Carl Landauer contribute "'Paint the Sunlight and All the Dark Corners Too': The Art of Lawrence Ferlinghetti." The Landauers review the phases in Ferlinghetti's career, including his sketching in France, his work as an Abstract Expressionist in San Francisco, and his works steeped in allusions to literature, art, and the careers of artists. Noting that Ferlinghetti's visual works feature recurring images of boats, birds, and artists, the Landauers form an interesting summary of Ferlinghetti: "In the matter of visual language, he understands that however many cultural references he marshals, his art must be intuited rather than intellectually processed" (47).

Like the Landauers, Melania Gazzotti and Anna Villari in "'Yet I Have Slept with Beauty in My Own Weird Way': The Memory of Europe in the Painting of Lawrence Ferlinghetti" make note of the main phases in Ferlinghetti's career as a visual artist. However, Gazzotti and Villari pay special attention to Ferlinghetti's early travels in Europe (1947-1950), claiming that "[i]t's a wealth of images, works, styles and—also using an academic term—of European Art History that settles in his memory, to re-emerge in his paintings often in an irreverent and ironic way" (53).

In addition to these critical observations, *60 Years of Painting* includes lively contributions from Rita Bottoms, Ferlinghetti's old friend from the University of California, Santa Cruz, and Elisa Polimeni, one of the editors of the volume. Bottoms remarks, "For decades Ferlinghetti has defied borders by embracing them as frontiers." She adds that "[i]n hundreds of his drawings and paintings, the women are poignant and haunting in their solitude, his male figures vulnerable and elusive, their longing palpable" (179). Polimeni describes the thrill of visiting Ferlinghetti's studio and unrolling canvases on the floor. Each canvas provokes a surge of emotion.

In all, *60 Years of Painting* is an indispensable collection. Ferlinghetti's works are now part of some of the most distinguished collections and exhibitions in the United States and around the world, but an oversized book such as *60 Years of Painting* provides simple access to Ferlinghetti's work to innumerable readers and viewers. Inspired by Ferlinghetti's vision, these readers and viewers may appreciate an artist of insightful compassion who insists on social justice.

---William Lawlor, *University of Wisconsin – Stevens Point*

Brother-Souls: John Clellon Holmes, Jack Kerouac, and the Beat Generation.
Ann Charters and Samuel Charters (Jackson: UP of Mississippi, 2010)

In February 1958, John Clellon Holmes wondered in his journal why he was not as widely known as Jack Kerouac and Allen Ginsberg. In fact, he began to wonder why he seemed to be excluded from general consideration as one of the Beat writers. He was, after all, one of Kerouac's closest friends who had been the first person to read *On the Road* as a fresh roll of typescript, who had published the first Beat Generation novel, *Go*, in 1952, and who had thereafter been asked to explicate the Beat ethos in a widely read *New York Times Magazine* essay. In the fall of 1961, University of California professor Thomas Parkinson published *A Casebook on the Beat* that included literary works by the now-expected cohort (Kerouac, Ginsberg, Gregory Corso, Lawrence Ferlinghetti, William S. Burroughs, etc.) and essays by the likes of Kenneth Rexroth, Norman Podhoretz, Warren Tallman, Herbert Gold, and others. Yet Parker included neither Holmes' literature nor his commentary.

As the Beat mystique grew in the years following Kerouac's death in 1969, Holmes was resurrected in the roles of observer and commentator, providing details in interviews and essays on a group of writers and confederates whose past was hazed over by alcohol and drugs, faulty memories, and the mythologizing consequences of legends told and retold. Holmes came to be seen as a less galvanizing writer than Kerouac had been, yet at the same time as a more reasonable chronicler of events. Some of the qualities that vitalized Kerouac as an enthralling book writer – his unrestrained and uninhibited literary manners – were the very qualities that made him unsuitable to serve the media as a spokesperson for his generation, let alone for his coterie of writers. Newspapers and magazines and soon biographers and scholars looked to Holmes for his reportage and his insights, since he had been an intimate part of the scene but did not seem to live the Beat lifestyle to the point that it rendered him incapable of producing considerate responses to their queries. Biographer Barry Miles declared that even in the late 1940s Holmes had been capable of navigating both the New York intelligentsia circles and the hipster world – and perhaps for that reason was never really fully integrated in either. Miles granted that Holmes possessed "a writer's eye for detail," but concluded that Holmes was "ultimately square and professorial, as his later career showed" (122). The general tone had been sounded earlier by Dennis McNally, another Kerouac biographer who, as became the norm, looked to Holmes' observations and records in order to amplify Kerouac's background and personality, while giving Holmes rather short shrift. In McNally's view, Holmes in the late 1940s had been an "angular young man," "a cerebral, analytical Massachusetts Yankee, [who] was also a writer." Not exactly the sort of description that brings the adoration of literature fans. Even Ann Charters' groundbreaking biography of Kerouac in 1973 portrayed a Holmes who was essentially a witness, not a catalyst, to the Beat scene.

John Clellon Holmes now gets a much fuller reckoning in Ann and Samuel Charter's full-length biography, *Brother-Souls: John Clellon Holmes, Jack Kerouac, and the Beat Generation*. In these pages Holmes emerges as an idealistic young man who spent the late 1940s shuffling between cheap New York City apartments, haggling over love affairs, wrestling with his soul, and struggling to be a writer. The Charters reveal the surprisingly key role that Holmes played in the development of Beat literature that has heretofore gone uncharted. More importantly, Holmes emerges as an important novelist whose work radiates a rhythm and force that equal those found in all the best Beat writing.

Most of the twenty-four chapters of the book begin with an excerpt from Holmes' unpublished journals or letters, and the pages throughout are laced with abundant selections from these sources. The result is that readers receive a weaving of the objective narrative text along with Holmes' own private voice. The Charters smoothly blend their storyline with the close observations of Holmes and occasionally of others as well, including Jay Landesman. Readers are always kept aware of who is making the observation, and whether the observations are contemporary with the scenes they accompany or are later reminiscences. Scenes are not presented as gospel, but as reportage from specific sources, a careful attentiveness that is often lacking in biographies where later recountings and novelized versions are incorporated at face value. The authors' reliability allows them to build a strong case for Holmes' inclusion as a Beat writer of the first rank.

Before either Kerouac or Ginsberg had found an audience, Holmes published poems in respectable journals, including *Partisan Review*, *Poetry*, *Chicago Review*, *Saturday Review of Literature*, and *Harper's*. In fact, he touted Ginsberg to Delmore Schwartz at *Partisan Review* in 1950, certainly a nugget of the Beat past that most readers would never have known. Readers who have availed themselves of the various collections of letters certainly would have known of Holmes' support for Kerouac in the early days, especially as he encouraged him to focus on his road material. But their relationship was far more complex and Holmes' influence was far more convoluted and consequential. In the closing weeks of 1950, a few months before Kerouac began hammering on the typescript that would become *On the Road*, he received a letter from Neal Cassady, referred to ever after as the "Joan Anderson letter," that Kerouac claimed was an American literary masterpiece. Little did Kerouac know, according to the Charters, that Holmes had been carrying on his own correspondence with Cassady, and one month earlier had sent Cassady his "Fay Kenney letter," to which Cassady responded with "Wooooooooo ooooooooooooooooooooooooooooooooo—EEEE! A real whiz of a letter" (179). A boomerang effect followed. After running out of steam on a short letter of reply to Holmes, Cassady promised to continue the tale of his own parallel adventures in person when he came back to New York City. Here the Charters take up the story: "Cassady's subsequent letter to Kerouac was written ten days later. The account of the 'Joan Anderson' hospital visit and the sexual exploits that followed read like a continuation of the letter Cassady had begun writing to Holmes" (179). When Kerouac showed Holmes the "Joan Anderson letter," Holmes recognized its debt to his own "Fay Kenney letter."

In addition to this and other cases for Holmes' influence, the biography also sheds light on Kerouac's famous twenty-day typing stint in April 1951, when he produced *On the Road*. Typically one imagines him sitting up all night, focused determinedly on his task. Holmes' journals make known a different scene: Kerouac's days passed apparently much like the days before and after the typing stint. Kerouac spent one long afternoon drinking with Holmes and went out for big drinking parties on at least several other occasions. That is, he remained social in his fashion. The three weeks of typing culminated nonetheless in a style in which Kerouac, Holmes believed, had found his voice. One note here: The Charters quote a journal Holmes' dated April 9, 1951, inserting the editorial "[sic]" when Holmes refers to the typescript as "a series of sixteen foot rolls of thin tracing paper" (192). They claim in their narrative of events that in fact the rolls of paper were ten feet long. It turns out, however, that Holmes was right, and the biographers are wrong.

This quibble is borne out by a prevalent structural device in the book. Although the full title of *Brother-Souls* suggests an equivalence of presentation between the two writers, readers are treated to a far more intimate perspective of Holmes than they are of Kerouac. Holmes' angst, motivations, and reactions are all abundantly illustrated with the immediacy of his journal entries and letters, and colored by the tints of his memoirs and reflections, all fully footnoted. Kerouac's life, on the other hand, is characterized by second- and third-hand summaries, without documentation. The result is a richer, fuller, treatment of Holmes. The two men's youthful lives are told in the initial stages of the book, and while their lives in some ways are on parallel arcs (they shared a birthday, four years apart, for one thing), the book threatens to bog down in a back-and-forth storyline. The pace and tone change considerably once the two men meet on a steamy July 4th weekend in 1948, but one might wonder whether Kerouac had been relied on to buoy Holmes' status, to maintain interest in the life of one who, as is the case for many others, is of interest to Kerouac readers because of his association with him. As the middle chapters unfold, this is clearly not the case, and Holmes' story captivates the reader without the obligation of Kerouac's erstwhile obligatory presence. Holmes comes forward as the principal subject, and Kerouac as an object of Holmes' perception.

One of the rewards of reading biographies, beyond exploring the life of the central figure, is that one is given the chance to discover the fascinating figures who are nonetheless tangential to that life, and here one is amply rewarded. Gershon Legman, the folklorist of eroticism, is without doubt among the most memorable of these characters. The description of a visit to his apartment is a masterpiece of evocation. So, too, are the characterizations of Jay and Fran Landesman and also, to a lesser extent, are those of Edward Stringham and Alan Harrington. Furthermore, readers are treated to an insider's view of jazz and the emergent be-bop trends. One of the true pleasures of this book is that that the streets and taverns and jazz joints of New York City in the late 1940s and 1950s come to life with the rhythms and sounds of daily life of the young bohemians as they argued about love, music, ideology, and literature.

Brother-Souls surpasses the obligation of exploring Holmes' life and times. The book supplies much-welcomed critical analyses of Holmes' novels *Go* and *The Horn* with a subtlety and surety befitting two seasoned scholars of music, literature, and the Beat Generation. These critically sympathetic readings of each novel will surely attract new readers to their pages and send old readers back to their bookshelves. In fact, *Brother-Souls* makes an extravagant claim for the future of *The Horn*, which at this time is apparently out of print: "It is not too much to assume that Holmes' novel will finally be accepted, like Kerouac's *On the Road*, as a modern American classic" (290). This is not bluster; the book argues the case convincingly.

Another prophecy can be made. *Brother-Souls* relies on a deep, meticulously kept, untapped archive of boyhood diaries, journals, notebooks, manuscripts, and correspondence that are stored in the Mugar Library at Boston University. It is time for John Clellon Holmes to have a rank of dedicated scholars who will see to the publication of and commentary on this rich reserve of American literature. And as this field develops and Holmes gets the recognition he deserves, this first-rate biography by Ann and Samuel Charters will be seen as the groundbreaking volume. Their book has been beautifully produced by the University Press of Mississippi in a high-quality binding, with extensive end notes, comprehensive bibliography, and thorough index. Superb research, clear, evocative writing, and professional packaging combine to distinguish John Clellon Holmes as a respected and important writer. *Brother-Souls* is a major work.

---Matt Theado, *Gardner-Webb University*

Works Cited

McNally, Dennis. *Desolate Angel: Jack Kerouac, the Beat Generation, and America*. New York: Random House, 1979.

Miles, Barry. *Jack Kerouac King of the Beats: A Portrait*. New York: Henry Holt, 1998.

The Etiquette of Freedom: Gary Snyder,
Jim Harrison, and The Practice of the Wild.
Edited by Paul Ebenkamp (Berkeley, CA: Counterpoint, 2010)

The wild requires that we learn the terrain, nod to all the plants and animals and birds, ford the streams and cross the ridges and tell a good story when we get back home (Gary Snyder, The Etiquette of Freedom [55])

Gary Snyder's voice resounds across the long shot of the vast Pacific Ocean in the establishing shot of John J. Healey's new film *The Practice of the Wild*. The encompassing wild wave of the ocean is a transcendental cipher in both the transcendentalist movement and East Asian Buddhisms, both important in Snyder's work, signifying for the former, nature's sublimity, and for the latter, awakened mind. Healey then shows us scenes from both the urban and rural landscapes, foreshadowing Snyder's comments about the importance of understanding nature not in the exclusive sense of The Great Outdoors, but inclusively as everything within the known universe, much as physicists do.

The Etiquette of Freedom: Gary Snyder, Jim Harrison, and The Practice of the Wild is a valuable book that can be seen a companion text to the film. *The Practice of the Wild* is the centerpiece of the project. The film is a brief (52 minutes) composition of black-and-white film footage and photos, smatterings of conversation between Snyder and Harrison, conversation around the dinner table with others, Snyder reading some of his better known poems, and reminiscences by Joanne Kyger, Michael McClure, Jack Shoemaker, with critical statements by Scott Slovic. Fans of Snyder will enjoy the black-and-white footage of him on his motorbike in 1950s San Francisco, complete with "end the war" inscribed on the oil cover just below the seat and gas tank, and his reading of "Hay for the Horses" which segues, in a nice bit of editing, with the author reading it in a clean, sparse, well-lit room. While I enjoyed these moments in the film, the most interesting and sometimes poignant moments occur in the flashes of conversation between Snyder and Harrison.

In their excerpted conversations around which all the other filmic elements revolve, Snyder and Harrison touch upon many of the themes familiar to readers of Snyder's work over the last 50 years; however, those new to Snyder will not feel lost because the way in which the two authors converse is casual and exoteric rather than formal and esoteric. I have to say, though, that there is a moment in the film when Harrison is asking Snyder about the recent death of Snyder's wife, Carole, and Snyder tells him that he wrote a poem about it and that he will show Harrison at a later date. It feels as though I am spying on the two men at an intimate moment but with a conflicting desire to see/hear the poem. This moment in the film opens a new view of Snyder in which we have not seen him before. The intimacy of Snyder's responses is due, in part, to the deep questions posed by Harrison.

While the film as a whole does not add to the scholarly appraisal of Snyder's work, some scholars may be interested in the discussion between Snyder and Harrison about the origin of the "How Poetry Comes to Me" poems that emerged on a two day hike in the Sierra Nevada Mountains. This now-famous trip became the basis for Jack Kerouac's 1958 novel, *The Dharma Bums*, in which Snyder is fictionally portrayed as Japhy Ryder, the "great new hero of American culture" (32). Snyder recalls that the poem "came to me, actually, camping one night in the Northern Sierra, and it actually happened the night that I went up that peak on the Northern Sierra boundary line, the Matterhorn, with Jack Kerouac" (61).

The film's extra features are worth mentioning as they contain additional remarks, in the case of the commentators, and the full reading that Snyder gave for the film of which only a few poems were used. My only criticism of the use of commentators is that there is not more use of Kyger and McClure in the film; however, what we do have are some thoughtful, personal and critical observations by Kyger, McClure and Shoemaker. The critical literary comments offered by Slovic are useful if the viewer is not familiar with the environmental and philosophical context of Snyder's work. In other words, there's not a lot here for seasoned Snyder scholars. Yet I do not think that the filmmakers and producers are aiming for a critical study of Snyder. Producer Will Hearst, in his "Foreword" to *The Etiquette of Freedom*, suggests that the idea of the film was to put Harrison and Snyder together and let "the story of Gary's life and how he came to think the way he does [emerge] from their conversations" (viii).

As the titles of both the film and book suggest, Snyder's collection of essays, *The Practice of the Wild*, is the reference point for the project. Hearst tells us that he first contacted Snyder when he "was the editor and publisher of *The Examiner*, in San Francisco" (vi). He invited Snyder to submit a piece for the Op-Ed page and the author sent him "The Etiquette of Freedom" later published as the lead essay in *The Practice of the Wild* (vi). It was Harrison who initially suggested to Hearst that Snyder would make a good subject for a documentary. So, the film, the book, and the direct use of *The Practice of the Wild* are set into a kind of dialogue with each other that speaks not only to Hearst's and Harrison's interest in Snyder but also long-standing themes in the author's life work.

Editor Paul Ebenkamp constructs *The Etiquette of Freedom* in four parts with the definitions of wild at the beginning of the text proper[1]. Part One is entitled "Working Landscapes" and is an interesting assemblage of conversation not included in the film, quotes taken from the various essays comprising *The Practice of the Wild*, quotes from thirteenth-century Soto Zen Master Dogen (1200-1253),[2] and a few black-and-white photographs from the years 1940-1986. Part Two is a transcript of the film that includes stills taken during the making of the film (these are also available on *The Practice of the Wild* Facebook page). Part Three is entitled "Further Talks" and includes outtakes from the Snyder-Harrison conversation as well as a sub-section entitled "Outtakes" with further comments from Shoemaker, Kyger, McClure, and Slovic. Part Four contains all the poems that Snyder reads both during the film and as an extra feature on the DVD. Ebenkamp also includes a *"Biographies and Reading Lists"* section for both Snyder and Harrison which will be a major help for those coming to one or both of these writers for the first time.

My only complaint is that the film is too short. Maybe it is because I love to hear Snyder speak and hear his insights that I write this. But there are some thought-provoking moments of conversation, such as Snyder's explanation of what he means by nature, and his comments on Zen Buddhism, that make the book but are excised from the final cut of the film. Maybe this is why we are offered both film and book. The book acts as a supplement to the film, and because it is primarily the transcript of the film plus outtakes it makes an excellent companion for those looking for more substance than the film offers. The two work together enlarging our understanding of Snyder and how those closest to him have understood him and his work through the years. One might say, as I am tempted to do here, that the film is a brief portrait of a man, poet, essayist, and teacher who has lived his life in an attempt to do something about the environmental crisis we have been in and to make himself native to his place—what Snyder has called, since the 1970s, reinhabition. By the end of the film, however, what was more apparent to me was the phenomenon of death and impermanence.

Watching Snyder and Harrison walking and talking and also seeing Kyger and McClure prompted a sense of grief in me. These people whom I have been reading for such a long time are aging! The sparkle is still in their respective eyes and voices, but the tell-tale signs of the passing of time is writ large on their bodies. So, it seemed appropriate to roll the credits and have the last topic of conversation be about death, aging, and Zen Buddhist conceptions of non-identity. It is appropriate to end the film with Snyder reading "They're Listening," a poem that challenges us to think not in terms of the short range of temporality, but in the long range of geologic time—giving us a longer view of life that exceeds yet includes individual experiences of time.

---Tom Pynn, *Kennesaw State University*

Notes

[1] This text appears in the essay "The Etiquette of Freedom" (*Practice* 9-10).

[2] Gary Snyder has made a recording of selections from Dogen's *Shobogenzo* ("moon in a dewdrop"), entitled *Zen Teachings of Zen Master Dogen*. Phoenix Audio. Abridged Edition, 2008.

Works Cited

Kerouac, Jack. *The Dharma Bums*. New York: Penguin, 1986.

Loori, John Daido. "River Seeing the River." *Dharma Rain: Sources of Buddhist Environmentalism*. Ed. Stephanie Kaza and Kenneth Kraft. Boston: Shambhala, 2000. 141-150.

---. *The Practice of the Wild*. San Francisco: North Point, 1990.

Tanahashi, Kazuaki, Trans. and Ed. *moon in a dewdrop: writings of zen master dogen*. New York: North Point, 1995.

Be Always Converting, Be Always Converted: An American Poetics.
Rob Wilson (Cambridge, MA: Harvard UP, 2009)

Beat Attitudes: On the Roads to Beatitude for Post-Beat Writers, Dharma Bums, and Cultural Activists.
Rob Sean Wilson (Santa Cruz, CA: New Pacific Press, 2010)

Tell all the Truth but tell it slant—
Success in Circuit lies
Too bright for our infirm

Delight The Truth's superb surprise
As Lightning to the Children eased
With explanation kind
The Truth must dazzle gradually
Or every man be blind—

In this poem Emily Dickinson discloses her justification for her approach to poetry. People, she cautions, need to be eased into truth or else they might be blinded. One familiar story literally bears out this phenomenon. On the road to Damascus, the recently executed Jesus appears to confront Saul, a persecutor of Christians. Jesus' radiance knocks Saul to the ground: "And Saul arose from the earth; and when his eyes were opened, he saw no man: but they led him by the hand, and brought him into Damascus. And he was three days without sight, and neither did eat nor drink" (Acts 9:8-9). "Seeing the light" is a metaphor for a conversion experience that can be a relatively minor affair ("So that's why my car won't start!") or a soul-shaking event, as with Saul, who, regaining his sight, dropped his Greek name and became Paul, one of history's greatest evangelist. It is with this latter manner of conversion that Rob Wilson, professor of literature at the University of California, Santa Cruz, concerns himself in *Be Always Converting, Be Always Converted.* Wilson describes from numerous perspectives the particularly American ability to change one's spiritual perception, to adopt new views and beliefs that alter not only one's own outlook but the geopolitical landscape as well. For Wilson, conversion is not the completion of an act, but an act in process that potentially leads to re-version and counterconversion. Beat Studies scholars will be interested in the book's treatment of Bob Dylan as well as in the book's thorough and thoughtful integration of Beat ideals and Beatitude into Wilson's exploration of conversion, particularly in regard to Beat Studies' recent forays into transnationalism and geopolitics.

Conversion references percolate through the American idiom: "I am turning over a new leaf," "he is a new man," "she is a changed woman," "let's put the past behind us," and so on. A common aspect of these makeovers is that they take place within the individual, yet the capability of these conversions to regenerate individual lives represents a larger phenomenon of the democratic vista – America is fixated on and may be defined by conversion experiences. Wilson writes that "truckers, farmers, black nationalists, tattoo artists, boxers, confessional poets, baseball stars, supreme court justices, presidents, dharma bums, and economic hit men are all too driven by the tropes and dreams, energies, stories, codes, and sedimented figurations of the American religious imagination" (2). Wilson explores the nature of religious conversion and its effects on transnational affinities, American empire, as well as interior and individual processes of self-awareness. To illustrate his examination, he draws on the lives and writings of four figures who are widely divergent in terms of background and biography, but who each serve Wilson's purpose to demonstrate the effects of the conversion experience both personally and in larger contexts.

Wilson's task is a tough one; to paraphrase Raymond Carver, what do we talk about when we talk about conversion? Are there phenomenological studies of conversion experiences; are there available field studies that chart and assess the changes one goes through? Or, as is more likely, is Wilson grappling here with describing the indescribable, and therefore resorting to a technique of all-inclusiveness in order to avoid delimiting the expansiveness of his subject? What I mean by this is that Wilson pulls out all the stops, opens the floodgates, lets it fly, and not just occasionally, but on every page. When it comes to his sentences, he is a member in high standing of the everything-and-the-kitchen-sink club of writers. After opening the covers of his book, I found myself mystified after several pages of torrential prose in the introduction. When I arrived at the thesis, I hoped that this portion of the introduction would clarify and focus his point. I am not sure that it does, but you can decide for yourself:

> This book aims to show through its intensive focus on an eclectic (yet carefully chosen) range of postcolonial converts, from Henry 'Opukaha'ia (the first Native Hawaiian convert), to Bob Dylan (Jeremiac troper of the American polity), the Tongan novelist Epeli Hau'ofa's counterformation into a transracial ecumene he calls "Oceania," and Ai (Afro-American-Japanese poet and maker of frontier violence and racial masks), that the —born-again experience can open up a language of possibility, metamorphosis, transregional migration, cultural unsettling, and geopolitical becoming that is much more unstable, open-ended, and world-shattering – as an event of social transformation and self-reinscription – than any doctrinaire account of religious conviction, semiotic certainty, colonized subjection, or ideological fixity would suggest. (3)

Indeed. I will not say that I am not excited by the possibilities he outlines. I am always willing to follow an enthusiastic guide, but I will admit that I was not entirely sure just where we were headed. I marvel at Wilson's fluidity, his erudition, his vocabulary, and his ability to build a construction that leads his reader to the periodic point of his statement. Having read the book, I can now go back and see the ways in which this vitally positioned sentence indicates the direction he will take, but quite a bit of Dickinson's "tell-it-slant" admonition remains apparent. When we piece together the meaning of this sentence (and it is important that we do since it announces itself as the proposal of the study), we may conclude that the result of the examination of these four "postcolonial converts" will be a realization of the "language of possibility" (right?) that "is more unstable, open-ended" than "any doctrinaire account." But upon re-reading the sentence (and I have done so many times), we could also conclude that not only the language but also the "metamorphosis, transregional migration, cultural unsettling" are also necessarily parts of the catalogue of conversion effects that go beyond doctrinaire accounts. But if this were the case, then the catalogue's main verb could not be "is," which it is; it would be "are," which it is not. So readers are challenged to make choices in deciding the meaning of the sentence, which they ought not have to do. I only go to these lengths to demonstrate the method readers (or at least this reader) had to undergo in order to process Wilson's points, not only here, but on every page of the book.

Though often obscure and ambiguous, Wilson's ambitious prose does serve to convey his depth of feeling for the significance of effects of conversion in the postcolonial period. After several stumbling attempts to read the book, I chided myself, not Wilson, for my difficulty in following the study. I liked what he was getting at, I sensed a kinship with a fellow traveler, and I sensed he was expressing an inclusiveness of spiritual sharing that helps us to see history and politics as emanations of personal inner transformations. Plus, you can learn quite a lot from Wilson, who dispenses his copious knowledge of Pacific culture and history and establishes the context for the significance of 'Opukaha'ia and Hau'ofa and their after-effects. Predictably he refers to Emerson, but also to a galaxy of other figures, including Muhammad Ali, Charles Baudelaire, Kenneth Burke, Johnny Cash, Charlie Chaplin, Ann Coulter, Gilles Deleuze, Ernest Fenollosa, Billy Graham, Woody Guthrie, Greil Marcus, Herman Melville, and on and on. Wilson frequently weaves in references to Beatitude and to Beat poetics, citing such Beat writers as Allen Ginsberg, Robert Duncan, William Everson, William S. Burroughs, Phillip Lamantia, Albert Saijo, Gary Snyder, and, predominantly, Jack Kerouac. The book is probably brilliant, and maybe that is why I am somewhat blinded by its message.

According to the introductory notes, *Beat Attitudes*, published by New Pacific Press, "comprises an open-ended glossary and archive of citations and sayings expressing various meanings of 'beatitude' at the core of the Beat cultural-political and literary attitude: an unfinished archive broad and implicative, with sayings that emanate about and from states of written and acted-upon beatitude" (2). One can open this small book, about the dimensions of one of those bus-station rack paperbacks of bygone days, to any page and find snatches of prose and poetry from throughout history that reflect a theme of Beatness. If you happen to open the book to page 105, you will find excerpts from Pamela Lu, William Blake, Albert Saijo, and William Wordsworth, interesting gatherings of thoughts coming together out of happenstance that challenge or reinforce one another.

Wilson supplies occasional editorial comments, insights, and bridges among writers and ideas. The book concludes solidly with the Beatitudes of Jesus in the Sermon on the Mount. For readers who wish to track the quotations to their published sources, Wilson provides a comprehensive list of works cited.

Readers should avail themselves of this list of works, too, since unfortunately the quotations in the book cannot be trusted for accuracy. According to Wilson, when Jack Kerouac appeared on William F. Buckley's TV show in 1968, he defended his original conception of the Beat Generation, complaining that "in the papers they called it 'beat rioting' and 'beat insurrection.'" Kerouac actually said "beat mutiny," not "beat rioting." According to Wilson, John Clellon Holmes' "This Is the Beat Generation" contains this:

> A man is beat when he goes broke, and wagers the sum of his resources on a single number; and the young generation has done that from early youth. (84)

What Holmes published in the *New York Times Magazine* in 1952 was this:

> A man is beat whenever he goes for broke and wagers the sum of his resources on a single number; and the young generation has done that continually from early youth. (44)

Overall, the book is a fine guide for meditative reading and is a cache of spiritually affirming resources for those of us who like to flip a book open to a random page and be surprised.

---Matt Theado, *Gardner-Webb University*

Work Cited

Holmes, John Clellon. "This Is the Beat Generation." *The Beats: A Literary Reference* . Ed. Matt Theado. New York: Carroll & Graf, 2003: 43-46.

Kerouac at Bat: Fantasy Sports and the King of the Beats.
Isaac Gewirtz (The New York Public Library, 2009)

Sports have always played a central role in defining and contesting what it means to be American. During the first half of the twentieth century as the United States carved out its cultural and political identity, sports reflected anxieties surrounding shifting definitions of citizenship, region, and nation. From African-American Jack Johnson's victory over Caucasian James J. Jeffries in 1910 and the ensuing race riots, to President Franklin Delano Roosevelt delaying a press conference for Seabiscuit's victory over Horse of the Year War Admiral in 1938, to the "shot heard 'round the world" as the Giants beat the Dodgers in 1951, sports served as markers of progress and hope, throwing into relief both the fragmentations of the modern era and a lasting adherence to communal values.

Kerouac at Bat: Fantasy Sports and King of the Beats, by Isaac Gewirtz, speaks to the power of sports in our national consciousness by excavating their influence during this period on one of our great American writers, Jack Kerouac. As curator of the Berg Collection at The New York Public Library—now home to the Jack Kerouac Archive—Gewirtz employs his archival expertise to detail a lesser known trajectory of Kerouac's writerly mind: an elaborate world of fantasy sports, primarily baseball and horse racing, documented in handwritten and typed newsletters and broadsides that Kerouac began during his teenage years. Kerouac's interest in sports is no surprise: much has been made of his football scholarship to Columbia University, for example, a fact often invoked to represent his homegrown, all-American side. Baseball, horse racing, and boxing were all prominently featured in the Lowell daily newspaper of Kerouac's youth and, as Gewirtz explains, Kerouac's father Leo was an avid fan of sports (even supplementing his income as linotype operator at the Sullivan Brothers printing firm by producing large racing forms for display). Gewirtz argues that for Kerouac "sporting events glowed with the innocent promise of an idealized America, even as they recalled ancient, bloody rites of passage" (7). Recognizing that other writers have mythologized competitive sports, Gewirtz astutely understands that what makes Kerouac's interest unique, as manifested in the fantasy sports culture he created, is its degree of focus, even, one might say, obsessiveness.

At the age of fourteen, Kerouac created a baseball league and carefully charted the histories of the players, coaches, managers, and owners, including financial statistics and stories about player trades. In early versions, he began games by hitting a marble with a toothpick and eventually created a set of cards using a statistical system that estimated the outcome of each pitch based on the skills of batters and pitchers. At times, he incorporated actual pitching by throwing a projectile at a diagrammed board. Naming the teams after automobiles until the mid-1940s and then switching to color names (e.g., the Chicago Chryslers and the Boston Grays, respectively), Kerouac's unique flair for pop cultural humor emerges in the detailed biographical histories of players who have names like "Wino Love," "Loop Paige," "Warby Pepper," and "Zagg Parker," the latter taken from a nickname given to Kerouac during his teenage years to honor his "zigzagging" speed on the football field. Like real leagues, Kerouac's underwent changes—cities lost and regained teams, rosters and batting orders changed—and each season included an All-Star Game and a World Series. Using the name "Jack Lewis," an Anglicized version of his French name, Jean-Louis, Kerouac employed an alter ego who functioned alternately as player, manager, and reporter for *Jack Lewis's Baseball Chatter*. As a jockey in Kerouac's fantasy horse racing, Lewis had a family, complete with a wealthy wife who owned a horse farm and a son named Tad who was "expected to become a greater jockey than his immortal dad" (Gewirtz 29).

While the fantasy thoroughbred games only lasted, according to the available archival material, until Kerouac was sixteen, the colorful stories that flesh out these games in the hyperbolic sports writing style of his era suggest a substantial commitment that seems on par with his devotion to baseball. He wrote thorough background stories about races at imaginary New England tracks, including information about the horses, jockeys, trainers, and owners, sometimes using clippings of real horses on his news sheets, which included track conditions and weather. Kerouac enacted these games by releasing marbles and a ball bearing down a Parcheesi board and recording his results. The ball bearing, which traveled faster than the marbles, became known as the unparalleled horse Repulsion, "King of the Turf," who triumphantly beat his rival Gunwale. As in the section devoted to Kerouac's baseball leagues, the narrative arc of the thoroughbred racing comes to life in Gewirtz's adept presentation of the publications, including concise yet informative annotations for the reader.

Kerouac at Bat is most gratifying when Gewirtz traces the ways in which the fantasy teams intersected with Kerouac's literature and his approach to the world at large. With respect to the latter, Kerouac named his center fielder for the Boston Fords "Pancho Villa," after the Mexican revolutionary leader, and the pitcher of the Chicago Nashes "Rob Roy," after the Scottish folk hero and outlaw Robert Roy MacGregor, displaying his affinity for the bandits and revolutionaries of history. Accommodating changes in the national make-up of the sport after Jackie Robinson broke the color barrier in 1947, Kerouac added a black Cuban shortstop to the Philadelphia Pontiacs in 1949, calling him "El Negro." Even more fascinating is the subtle dialogue that emerges between Kerouac's teams and his literary works. In the 1950s, for instance, he called New York Greens pitcher "Pic," the name of a character who first appeared in a proto-version of *On the Road* in 1949 and eventually became the protagonist of the novella *Pic*. In another example, "Cody," the name that Kerouac used for Neal Cassady in early experimental versions of *On the Road*, which eventually became *Visions of Cody*, first surfaced as early as 1936 in "Phegie Cody," a pitcher for the Chicago Nashes.

The texts that Gewirtz compiles using only a small percentage of the available documents convincingly showcase fantasy sports as an integral component of Kerouac's oeuvre. The imaginative scope of Kerouac's painstaking verisimilitude resonates strongly for the reader. However, while *Kerouac at Bat* implicitly makes a solid case for the value of archival work in understanding Kerouac as a writer, what is missing is sustained scrutiny that could illuminate the point of all of this. This rich source material begins to come to life when Gewirtz ruminates on what propelled Kerouac into such a lifelong obsession, but his answer—escape and refuge—barely scratches the surface. In particular, he turns to Kerouac's trauma, resentment, and guilt over the death of his brother Gerard, who died at age nine when Kerouac was four. This is a specious argument at best. Creative expression rarely fits easily into systems of psychoanalytic causality, and Kerouac, rather than avoiding the most painful aspects of his life, confronted them repeatedly in his published work. The most compelling explanation that Gewirtz gives is that fantasy sports provided a kind of safe space from the embattled dualism that critics have long identified as an integral part of Kerouac's cultural and literary legacy, "his dichotomous, warring identities: small-town football hero versus sensitive, big-city artist; all-American writer versus fiercely proud Breton-Canuck, resentful of the Anglo culture in which he often felt like a despised stranger; warmth and generosity at war with embittered bigotry" (8). People with artistic impulses, however, always wade through conflicting notions of selfhood and belonging, and Kerouac channeled these tugs-of-war into every aspect of his life. Subterfuge wasn't his style.

Gewirtz offers revealing hints and shrewd gestures at analysis, but they fall short of the complexity that a careful reader might perhaps glean. His subtitle calls attention to the "King of the Beats" moniker that, along with the spotlight that attended it, proved problematic for Kerouac throughout his life. Is Gewirtz being a bit tongue in cheek? Does he want the reader immediately to sense the contradictory impulses that seem to attend Kerouac at bat and Kerouac the King? The brief explanations could go further. Escape, for example, doesn't tell us a whole lot. One could argue that any artist is always escaping, negotiating, and reframing his/her marginality in some way. What would be more useful is a probing look at the aspects of Kerouac's fantasy sport that seem unique: the meticulousness, for one. Why go to such great lengths to ensure that every aspect seems entirely plausible within the fantasy sports world itself, particularly when he was sharing this information with almost nobody? Yes, a good writer is first and foremost a good storyteller and Kerouac obviously felt impelled to sharpen this skill throughout his life, but he had numerous outlets for rehearsal, as evidenced in journals and multiple drafts of novels. If fantasy sports functioned as a hidden refuge, did it counterbalance his literary work, which often served as confession or exposure, or did it create a kind of escapist parallel universe, throwing into relief and deeply impacting his novels, poems, and essays? More importantly, what, ultimately, can these fantasy games reveal about Kerouac's writing—his spontaneous prose, his unique blend of fact and fiction, his Duluoz legend? Intentions, in other words, seem less interesting than how one might understand the larger implications.

It's clear that Gewirtz understands the value and impact of this creative output. In a *New York Times* review, for example, he says, "To me it's another indication of the kind of mind that allowed him to be the writer he was" (McGrath). Unlike the material that makes up *Beatific Souls*, however, which riffs on knowledge already existent in public conceptions of Kerouac as a result of scholarship by Ann Charters, Tim Hunt, George Dardess, and Howard Cunnell, among others, *Kerouac at Bat* gives us raw, undigested information in need of stewardship. A deeper investigation of the recycled character names, for instance, could help broaden our understanding of Kerouac's complex intertextual play, particularly when taking into account the fact that he kept his fantasy world almost completely secret. This decision is a striking one for a writer who wrote in his "Essentials of Spontaneous Prose" that "the best writing is always the most painful personal wrungout tossed from cradle warm protective mind tap from yourself the song of yourself, blow! now! your way is your only way 'good' or 'bad' always honest, ('ludicrous'), spontaneous, 'confessional' interesting, because not 'crafted'" (Kerouac 58). Kerouac's literature always encoded the reader and established a kind of pact in the writing itself. Even his private journals, which are excerpted in a volume that Douglas Brinkley edited, engage explicitly with public readers. His fantasy sports writing, however, implied a readership but remained almost exclusively within his own purview. This disparity unsettles our conceptions of what drove Kerouac to write and suggests new, as yet untheorized, interventions.

Throughout the book, Gewirtz hints at larger meaning. In a parenthetical afterthought regarding Repulsion's victory over Gunwale, for example, he explains, "Even at this early age, Kerouac realized that a true champion can achieve greatness only by defeating a great rival" (19). Similarly reflective when discussing the short-lived West Coast life of the fantasy teams, he remarks, "By 1961, and probably a year or two earlier, the California teams have disappeared, along with Kerouac's enchantment with the Golden State and his youthful, beatific vision of America's spiritual renewal" (39). These are hidden gems of critical thought and inquiry that leave the reader wanting more. How did Kerouac's competitive instinct infuse and shape his writing? Did he identify, in a sense, with Repulsion? One can't help but make the connection—in a quote from the unpublished *Memory Babe* scroll of 1958, which Gewirtz enlarges and sets off on its own page, Kerouac explains that he named his horse Repulsion "because I knew he would repulse all other horses forever . . . . Which he did" (22). To repulse is not merely to vanquish. It suggests a stronger sense of outsiderness as well as an active role in sustaining it, which gives insight into Kerouac's own vexed relationship with critics, friends, family members, and lovers throughout his life. Repulsion, the horse, resurfaces in *Doctor Sax* and thus remains a potent figure in Kerouac's literary imagination, a fact that Gewirtz never mentions. In the case of California serving as a barometer of Kerouac's disenchantment—a conclusion that needs supporting evidence—if these fantasy teams elucidate the fluctuations of Kerouac's belief in the promise of America, they can give us a lens through which to chart the course of his literary voice in ways that might prove refreshing and unexpected.

In a 1938 issue of *Jack Lewis's Baseball Chatter*, Kerouac wrote, at age sixteen, "Woe is Bob, the gum-chewing, apple seed chucker, and spontaneous individual who fills the seat in the office below the office of Edward Janke, Chevvy impresario. Didn't he have enough trouble with those Farr Flambasters already. Why do such people roam this land of liberty?" (Gewirtz 45). When discovering moments like these, readers of *Kerouac at Bat* feel a sense of wonder and intrigue, and find fertile terrain for reimagining Kerouac as a writer. Gewirtz is less concerned with theoretical exploration than with unveiling this virtually unknown side of Kerouac, which is a significant contribution, considering that the combined effect of an inaccessible archive and a caricatured literary movement has severely distorted our general understanding of Kerouac and relegated scholars of his work to a kind of dispossession. Because Gewirtz presents this material in an adroit manner, we have a new portal through which to examine one of the twentieth century's most important writers. Still, one can not help but wonder what *Kerouac at Bat* might have been as a collaborative effort conjoining archival work and in-depth critical evaluation. Then, when stumbling onto literary delights like the one above, readers could find signposts to help steer them through the startled sense of having arrived at the early stages of spontaneous bop prosody. On a broader level, we could find new strategies for investigating Kerouac's profound entrenchment in the potentialities of America.

---Penny Vlagopoulos – *Texas A&M International University*

Works Cited

Kerouac, Jack. "Essentials of Spontaneous Prose." *The Portable Beat Reader*. Ed. Ann Charters. New York: Penguin, 1992. 57-58. Print.

McGrath, Charles. "Another Side of Kerouac: The Dharma Bum as Sports Nut."
    New York Times. 16 May 2009. Web. 29 Aug. 2010.

The Beat Review Index

The following is a list of all reviews of Beat scholarship and literature from September 2007 -- the first issue of *The Beat Review* -- through February 2012. The *Journal of Beat Studies* will update the list annually. We hope that scholars find it a useful resource, one that illustrates the rich body of work in Beat Studies.

The Beat Review is available online at http://www.beatstudies.org/reviews/default.html

---

Abbott, Keith. *Downstream from Trout Fishing in America* (revised). Reviewed by John Whalen-Bridge (Volume 4, Issue 3).

Baker, Deborah. *A Blue Hand: The Beats in India.* Reviewed by Keith Abbott (Volume 2, Issue 4).

Baker, Phil. *William S. Burroughs.* Reviewed by Katharine Streip (Volume 4, Issue 3).

Ball, Gordon. *Films by Gordon Ball* (DVD video). Reviewed by Kurt Hemmer (Volume 5, Issue 1).

Ball, Gordon. *East Hill Farm: Seasons with Allen Ginsberg.* Reviewed by Marc Olmsted (Volume 6, Issue 1).

Buhle, Paul, ed. *The Beats: A Graphic History.* Text by Harvey Pekar, et al. Art by Ed Piskor et al. Reviewed by Matt Theado (Volume 3, Issue 2).

Burroughs, William S., and Jack Kerouac. *And the Hippos Were Boiled in Their Tanks.* Reviewed by Fiona Paton (Volume 3, Issue 1).

Burroughs, William S. *Everything Lost: The Latin American Notebook of William S. Burroughs.* Ed. Geoffrey D. Smith and John M. Bennett. Volume Ed., Oliver Harris. Reviewed by Jennie Skerl (Volume 2, Number 4).

Cassady, Neal. *Collected Letters: 1944-1967.* Reviewed by Jonah Raskin (Volume 2, Issue 1).

Charters, Ann, and Samuel Charters. *Brother-Souls: John Clellon Holmes, Jack Kerouac, and the Beat Generation.* Reviewed by Matt Theado (Volume 4, Issue 4).

Cohen, Mark, ed. *Missing a Beat: The Rants and Regrets of Seymour Krim.* Reviewed by Craig Svonkin (Volume 5, Issue 3).

Cohn, Jim. *Sutras & Bardos: Essays & Interviews on Allen Ginsberg, the Kerouac School, Anne Waldman, The Postbeat Poets & the New Demotics.* Reviewed by Jonah Raskin (Volume 5, Issue 3).

Conners, Peter. *White Hand Society: The Psychedelic Partnership of Timothy Leary & Allen Ginsberg.* Reviewed by Marc Olmsted (Volume 5, Issue 1).

Diano, Giada, and Elisa Polimeni, ed. *Lawrence Ferlinghetti (60 Years of Painting).* Reviewed by William Lawlor (Volume 4, Issue 3).

Diggory, Terence. *Encyclopedia of The New York School of Poets.* Reviewed by Tim Hunt (Volume 4, Issue 1).

Ebenkamp, Paul, ed. *The Etiquette of Freedom: Gary Snyder, Jim Harrison, and The Practice of the Wild.* Reviewed by Tom Pynn (Volume 5, Issue 1).

Edington, Stephen. *The Beat Face of God: the Beat Generation Writers as Spirit Guides.* Reviewed by Matt Theado (Volume 2, Issue 3).

Edington, Stephen. *Kerouac's Nashua Connection.* Reviewed by Matt Theado (Volume 2, Issue 3).

Epstein, Rob, and Jeffrey Friedman, dir. *Howl.* Reviewed by Kurt Hemmer (Volume 4, Issue 4).

Farrar, Jay, and Benjamin Gibbard. *One Fast Move or I'm Gone: Music from Kerouac's Big Sur.* CD. Reviewed by Tom Pynn (Volume 4, Issue 1).

Ferlinghetti, Lawrence. *A Coney Island of the Mind: Special 50th Anniversary Edition.* Reviewed by Tom Pynn (Volume 3, Issue 1).

Ferlinghetti, Lawrence. *Poetry as Insurgent Art.* Reviewed by Tom Pynn (Volume 3, Issue 1).

Geiger, John. *Nothing is True, Everything is Permitted: The Life of Brion Gysin.* Reviewed by Jennie Skerl (Volume 4, Issue 4).

Gewirtz, Isaac. *Beatific Soul: Jack Kerouac on the Road.* Reviewed by Ann Charters (Volume 2, Issue 1).

Gewirtz, Isaac. *Kerouac at Bat: Fantasy Sports and the King of the Beats.* Reviewed by Penny Vlagopoulos (Volume 4, Issue 3).

Ginsberg, Allen. *The Letters of Allen Ginsberg.* Ed. Bill Morgan. Reviewed by Jonah Raskin (Volume 2, Issue 4).

Ginsberg, Allen, and Gary Snyder. *The Selected Letters of Allen Ginsberg and Gary Snyder.* Ed. Bill Morgan. Reviewed by Jonah Raskin (Volume 3, Issue 1).

Grace, Nancy M. *Jack Kerouac and the Literary Imagination.* Reviewed by Fiona Paton (Volume 2, Issue 2).

Gray, Tim. *Gary Snyder and the Pacific Rim.* Reviewed by Keith Abbott (Volume 1, Issue 2).

Harris, Latif, and Neeli Cherkovski, ed. *Beatitude Golden Anniversary 1959-2009.* Reviewed by Chad Weidner (Volume 4, Issue 4).

Harris, Oliver, and Ian Macfadyen, ed. *Naked Lunch @ 50: Anniversary Essays.* Reviewed by Katharine Streip (Volume 3, Issue 2).

Harris, Oliver, ed. *Queer (25th Anniversary Edition)* by William S. Burroughs. Reviewed by Ryan Ehmke (Volume 5, Issue 3).

Hemmer, Kurt, and Tom Knoff. *Wow!—Ted Joans Lives!*; *Rebel Roar: The Sound of Michael McClure*; *As We Cover the Streets: Janine Pommy Vega* (DVD videos). Reviewed by Terence Diggory (Volume 5, Issue 1).

Hoffman, John. *Journey to the End.* Reviewed by Brian Jackson (Volume 2, Issue 2).

Holladay, Hilary, and Robert Holton. *What's Your Road, Man? Critical Essays on Jack Kerouac's* On the Road. Reviewed by Nancy M. Grace (Volume 3, Issue 2).

Hrebeniak, Michael. *Action Writing: Jack Kerouac's Wild Form.* Reviewed by Fiona Paton (Volume 1, Issue 2).

Hunt, Tim. *Kerouac's Crooked Road: The Development of a Fiction* (revised). Reviewed by Jonah Raskin (Volume 4, Issue 3).

Johnson, Rob. *The Lost Years of William S. Burroughs.* Reviewed by Jennie Skerl (Volume 1, Issue 1).

Jones, Hettie. *Doing 70.* Reviewed by Tony Trigilio (Volume 4, Issue 4).

Katz, Eliot. *Love, War, Fire, Wind: Looking Out from North America's Skull.* Drawings by William T. Ayton. Reviewed by Tony Trigilio (Volume 3, Issue 2).

Kerouac, Jack. *Book of Sketches*. Reviewed by Dave Moore (Volume 2, Issue 1).

Kerouac, Jack. *On the Road: The Scroll*. Reviewed by Matt Theado (Volume 1, Issue 2).

Kerouac, Jack. *Wake Up: A Life of the Buddha*. Reviewed by Jonah Raskin (Volume 2, Issue 4).

Kerouac, Jack, and Allen Ginsberg. *Jack Kerouac and Allen Ginsberg: The Letters*. Ed. Bill Morgan and David Stanford. Reviewed by Jonah Raskin (Volume 4, Issue 2).

Kerouac-Parker, Edie. *You'll Be Okay: My Life with Jack Kerouac*. Reviewed by Nancy M. Grace (Volume 1, Issue 2).

Kyger, Joanne. *About Now: The Collected Poems of Joanne Kyger*. Reviewed by Jonah Raskin (Volume 1, Issue 2).

Lamantia, Philip. *Tau*. Reviewed by Brian Jackson (Volume 2, Issue 2).

Lee, A. Robert. *Modern American Counter Writing: Beats, Outriders, Ethnics*. Reviewed by Jennie Skerl (Volume 4, Issue 2).

Leland, John. *Why Kerouac Matters: The Lessons of On the Road (They're Not What You Think)*. Reviewed by Tim Hunt (Volume 3, Issue 1).

Leyser, Yony. *William S. Burroughs: A Man Within* (DVD). Reviewed by Kurt Hemmer (Volume 6, Issue 1).

McClure, Michael. *Mysterioso and Other Poems*. Reviewed by Tom Pynn (Volume 4, Issue 2).

McClure, Michael. *Of Indigo and Saffron: New and Selected Poems* (ed. Leslie Scalapino). Reviewed by Tom Pynn (Volume 5, Issue 2).

Miller, Henry. *Sextet*. Reviewed by Tom Pynn (Volume 4, Issue 4).

Mills, Katie. *The Road Story and the Rebel: Moving Through Film, Fiction, and Television*. Reviewed by Jennie Skerl (Volume 3, Issue 1).

Morgan, Bill. *Beat Atlas: A State by State Guide to the Beat Generation in America*. Reviewed by Jimmy Fazzino (Volume 5, Issue 2).

Morgan, Bill. *I Celebrate Myself: The Somewhat Private Life of Allen Ginsberg*. Reviewed by Tony Trigilio (Volume 2, Issue 3).

Morgan, Bill. *The Typewriter is Holy: The Complete, Uncensored History of the Beat Generation*. Reviewed by Tom Pynn (Volume 4, Issue 3).

Mortenson, Erik. *Capturing the Beat Moment: Cultural Politics and the Poetics of Presence*. Reviewed by Phil Dickinson (Volume 5, Issue 1).

Nicosia, Gerald, ed. *Jan Kerouac: A Life in Memory*. Reviewed by Marc Olmsted (Volume 3, Issue 2).

Nicosia, Gerald, and Anne Marie Santos. *One and Only: The Untold Story of* On the Road *and of Lu Anne Henderson, the Woman Who Started Jack and Neal on Their Journey*. Reviewed by Nancy M. Grace (Volume 6, Issue 1).

Nock-Hee Park, Josephine. *Apparitions of Asia: Modernist Form and Asian American Poetics*. Reviewed by Jason G. Arthur (Volume 2, Issue 3).

Sandison, David, and Graham Vickers. *Neal Cassady—The Fast Life of a Beat Hero*. Reviewed by Steve Edington (Volume 2, Issue 2).

Smith, Patti. *Woolgathering*. Reviewed by Tom Pynn (Volume 6, Issue 1).

Snyder, Gary. *Back on the Fire*. Reviewed by Tom Pynn (Volume 3, Issue 2).

Snyder, Gary. *Passage Through India: An Expanded and Illustrated Edition*. Reviewed by Tom Pynn (Volume 3, Issue 2).

Stevens, Michael. *The Road to Interzone: Reading William S. Burroughs Reading*. Reviewed by Kurt Hemmer (Volume 3, Issue 3).

Tietchen, Todd F. *The Cubalogues: Beat Writers in Revolutionary Havana*. Reviewed by Phil Dickinson (Volume 4, Issue 4).

Trigilio, Tony. *Allen Ginsberg's Buddhist Poetics*. Reviewed by Tom Pynn (Volume 2, Issue 3).

Von Vogt, Elizabeth. *681 Lexington Avenue: A Beat Education in New York City, 1947-1954*. Reviewed by Amy Friedman (Volume 2, Issue 3).

Waldman, Anne. *In the Room of Never Grieve: New and Selected Poems, 1985-2003*. Reviewed by Todd Nathan Thorpe (Volume 3, Issue 3).

Waldman, Anne. *Manatee/Humanity*. Reviewed by Todd Nathan Thorpe (Volume 3, Issue 3).

Waldman, Anne. *Outrider*. Reviewed by Jane Falk (Volume 2, Issue 2).

Weaver, Helen. *The Awakener: A Memoir of Kerouac and the Fifties*. Reviewed by Jonah Raskin (Volume 3, Issue 2).

Weddle, Jeff. *Bohemian New Orleans: The Story of the Outsider and Loujon Press*. Reviewed by Nancy M. Grace (Volume 5, Issue 1).

Whalen-Bridge, John, and Gary Storhoff, ed. *The Emergence of Buddhist American Literature*. Reviewed by Tony Trigilio (Volume 3, Issue 3).

Whalen, Philip. *The Collected Poems of Philip Whalen*. Reviewed by Keith Abbott (Volume 2, Issue 1).

Wilson, Rob. *Be Always Converting, Be Always Converted: An American Poetics*. Reviewed by Matt Theado (Volume 5, Issue 2).

Wilson, Rob. *Beat Attitudes: On the Roads to Beatitude for Post-Beat Writers, Dharma Bums, and Cultural Activists*. Reviewed by Matt Theado (Volume 5, Issue 2).

Worden, Curt, dir. *One Fast Move or I'm Gone: Kerouac's Big Sur*. Reviewed by Tom Pynn (Volume 4, Issue 1).

Call for Essays for the *Journal of Beat Studies* #2: Beats and Naropa

Since 1974, the Naropa Institute (University) has been a proving ground for generations of Beat writers, serving to measure and extend the vitality of Beat poetics beyond the impact of the early Beat writers. This largely unexplored territory in the critical literature will be the focus of the second issue of the *Journal of Beat Studies*.

Essays in this issue will examine the critical role Naropa has played in the shaping of Beat poetics.

Essays could address the following:
- Individual Beat writers associated with Naropa
- Foundational Beat movement influences transmitted in the school
- The impact on poetics of the "Naropa wars" of the 1970s
- Explorations of the critical and literary significance of the "*On the Road*: The Jack Kerouac Conference" of 1982
- Beats and Buddhism
- Beats and Spiritual Excursions
- Naropa's effect on institutionalizing the Beats
- Naropa and transnational Beats poetic

Please consult style guidelines published in this issue and posted on the Beat Studies Association web site: http://www.beatstudies.org/jbs/index.html

Essays should be sent no later than July 1, 2012, to Ronna C. Johnson (ronna. johnson@tufts.edu) and Nancy M. Grace (Ngrace@wooster.edu) simultaneously.

Call for Proposals for the *Journal of Beat Studies #3*: Cambridge-Boston and the Rise of Beat Poetics

Incubation in the informal literary communities of Cambridge and Boston instilled rising Beat writing with local versions of Black Mountain and nascent New York School poetics. The Poets' Theater at Harvard University and Boston's Beacon Hill were pivotal locales in early Beat writing allowing surprising mutual influences and collaborations before the emergent literary schools and their associated poetics were solidified. Many Beat writers confronted dynamics of the movement's archetypal dilemma of status inclusion that was especially acute in the insider-outsider exclusivity of Cambridge-Boston. This area of study will be the focus of the third issue of the *Journal of Beat Studies*.

Essay proposals can address the following:
- Individual writers such as John Wieners, Charles Olson, V.R. ("Bunny") Lang, and Robert Creeley
- Gregory Corso's poetry and drama
- The influence of Allen Ginsberg or Jack Kerouac on emerging Beat poets in Cambridge-Boston
- The Poet's Theatre
- Poetry Readings at the Charles Street Meeting House
- Poet Isabella Gardner's Beat Connections

Proposals should be sent no later than September 1, 2012, to Ronna C. Johnson (ronna.johnson@tufts.edu) and Nancy M. Grace (Ngrace@wooster.edu) simultaneously.

Notes on Contributors

Jimmy Fazzino teaches in the literature, writing, and creative writing programs at the University of California, Santa Cruz. He has been a contributor to *The Beat Review* and has several articles on the Beats forthcoming in *The Literary Encyclopedia*. His most recent publication is "The Beat Manifesto: Avant-Garde Poetics and the Worlded Circuits of African American Beat Surrealism" in *The Transnational Beat Generation* (Palgrave 2012). Research interests include twentieth-century American literature and modern poetry and poetics. His dissertation is entitled "Beat Subterranean: Assemblages of Influence and Beat Writing in World Contexts."

Tim Hunt is a professor of English at Illinois State University in Normal, Illinois. He is a founding member of the Beat Studies Association and its current president. He is the author of *Kerouac's Crooked Road*, the editor of *The Selected Poetry of Robinson Jeffers* and *The Collected Poetry of Robinson Jeffers*. His most recent collection of poetry is *Fault Lines*, and he has published essays and given papers on textual mediation in modern American poetry. His current critical project is the book-length manuscript *Textual Subversion: Kerouac and the Advent of Post-Literacy Literature*, from which the essay in this volume is excerpted.

Bill Mohr is an associate professor in the Department of English at California State University, Long Beach. His creative and critical writing has appeared in dozens of magazines, including *Antioch Review*, *Blue Mesa Review*, *Caliban Online*, *Chicago Review*, *Santa Monica Review*, *Sonora Review*, *Spot Literary Magazine*, *William Carlos Williams Review*, *ZYZZYVA*, and *5 AM*. As editor of Momentum Press from 1974 to 1988, he received four grants from the National Endowment for the Arts and published two major anthologies of Southern California poets. His books of poetry and audio recording collections include *Hidden Proofs*, *Vehemence*, and *Bittersweet Kaleidoscope*. His literary history of the Los Angeles poetry scenes in the second half of the 20th century, *Hold-Outs: The Los Angeles Poetry Renaissance 1948-1992*, was published by the University of Iowa Press in 2011. Earlier installments of that project appeared in David James' *The Sons and Daughters of Los: Culture and Community in L.A.* (Temple University Press, 2003) and Kevin McNamara's *The Cambridge Companion to the Literature of Los Angeles* as well as *New Review of Literature*, edited by Paul Vangelisti.

Reviewers

Phil Dickinson is a lecturer and associate chair and undergraduate coordinator in the English Department at Bowling Green State University in Bowling Green, Ohio.

Ryan Ehmke teaches English at the Naval Academy Preparatory School in Newport, Rhode Island, and is a doctoral student at Florida State University in Tallahassee, Florida, focusing his study on the history of text technologies and twentieth-century literatures.

William Lawlor is a professor of English at the University of Wisconsin— Stevens Point and the author of *Beat Culture: Lifestyles, Icons, and Impact* and *The Beat Generation: A Bibliographical Teaching Guide*.

Marc Olmsted is a poet and the author of *Milky Desire*, *Resume,* and *What Use Am I a Hungry Ghost*.

Tom Pynn is an assistant professor of philosophy and coordinator of the Peace Studies Program at Kennesaw State University in Kennesaw, Georgia. He has published essays and book review essays on Jack Kerouac's Buddhism, Allen Ginsberg's Buddhist poetics, and yoga philosophy.

Jonah Raskin is a professor emeritus at Sonoma State University in Rohnert Park, California. He is the author of *American Scream: Allen Ginsberg's "Howl" and the Making of the Beat Generation* as well as many other books on American literature and culture.

Jennie Skerl is retired from West Chester University in West Chester, Pennsylvania, where she was associate dean of the College of Arts and Sciences. She has authored and edited a number of books on the Beats, including *William S. Burroughs*, *Reconstructing the Beats* (editor), and *The Transnational Beat Generation* (co-editor).

Matt Theado is an associate professor of English at Gardner-Webb University in Boiling Springs, North Carolina. He is the author of *The Beats: A Literary Reference* and *Understanding Jack Kerouac*.

Penny Vlagopoulos is an assistant professor of English at Texas A&M International University in Laredo, Texas. Her essay "Rewriting America: Kerouac's Nation of 'Underground Monsters'" was published in *On the Road: The Original Scroll*.

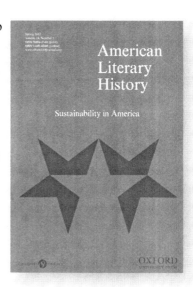

Tulsa Studies in Women's Literature

Publishing scholarship on women's writing for 30 years

SUBMIT

Guidelines at
...lsa.edu/tswl

College **Literature**

a journal of critical literary studies

Graham MacPhee, Editor

West Chester University
201 E. Rosedale Avenue
West Chester, PA 19383
Tel: 610.436.2901
collit@wcupa.edu

College Literature publishes innovative scholarship from across the various periods and fields that comprise the changing discipline of literary studies. The journal aims to scrutinize the theoretical parameters and assumptions underlying contemporary critical practice, and to examine the political and institutional limits that define the discipline.

http://www.wcupa.edu/_academics/sch_cas.lit/

MELUS

Multi-Ethnic Literature of the United States

PUBLISHED QUARTERLY, *MELUS* features articles, interviews, and reviews reflecting the multi-ethnic scope of American literature. Lively, informative, and thought-provoking, *MELUS* is a valuable resource for teachers and students interested in African American, Hispanic, Asian and Pacific American, Native American, and ethnically specific Euro-American works, their authors, and their cultural contexts.

INSTITUTIONS, colleges, universities, and libraries can subscribe to the journal for $120.00 per year for US institutions; the non-US institutional rate is $140.00. Checks payable to *MELUS* may be sent to the Editorial Office at *MELUS*, Department of English, U-4025, 215 Glenbrook Road, University of Connecticut, Storrs, CT 06269-4025. Institutions may also subscribe through PayPal at www.melus.org.

INDIVIDUAL SUBSCRIBERS become members of The Society for the Study of the Multi-Ethnic Literature of the United States. To subscribe, send a check payable to *MELUS* to Professor Georgina Dodge, Membership Chair, University of Iowa, 111 Jessup Hall, Iowa City, IA 52242 (georgina-dodge@uiowa.edu). Regular US membership is $50.00 per year; students and retirees, $30.00; regular non-US membership is $70.00; non-US students and retirees, $50.00. You may also subscribe through PayPal at www.melus.org.

For more information about submitting essays, ordering back issues, and placing advertisements, see www.melus.org or e-mail us at:
melus@uconn.edu

Policy

The *Journal of Beat Studies* invites articles on the works of Beat movement writers and their colleagues, especially New York School, Black Mountain School, and San Francisco Renaissance writers, as well as those connected to these movements, in the United States and globally. The *Journal* intends to represent the breadth and eclecticism of critical approaches to Beat generation writers, and welcomes new perspectives and contexts of inquiry.

Articles that are deemed appropriate are sent for review anonymously to a member of the Editorial Board and at least one other reader. Manuscripts should not be under consideration elsewhere and we do not publish previously published work. It is strongly advised that those submitting work to *JBS* be familiar with the journal's content. Among criteria on which evaluation of submissions depends are whether an article demonstrates recognition of and thorough familiarity with scholarship already published in the field, whether the article is written clearly and effectively, and whether it makes a genuine contribution to Beat studies.

Preparation of Copy

1. Articles are typically between 25 and 30 pages, and do not exceed 9000 words, including notes and works cited. Inquiries about significantly shorter or longer submissions should be sent to the editors.

2. A separate page should include the article's title, author's name, address, telephone & fax numbers, and e-mail address. The author's name and identifying references should not appear on the manuscript to preserve anonymity for our readers.

3. All submissions must include an abstract of no more than 250 words.

4. The manuscript should be in Times New Roman 12, double-spaced, and should adhere to the most recent MLA style.

5. Submissions may be sent by email as word documents ("doc" only, not "docx") to Ronna C. Johnson (ronna.johnson@tufts.edu) and Nancy M. Grace (ngrace@wooster.edu) simultaneously. Mailed submissions may be sent to Nancy M. Grace, Department of English, 400 E. University Street, The College of Wooster, Wooster, Ohio 44691. For mailed submissions, please send three copies of the article and abstract.

6. Submissions may also be sent via the online submission form at http://www.beatstudies.org/jbs/submission_guidelines.html.

7. Authors of accepted manuscripts are responsible for any necessary permissions fees and for securing any necessary permissions.

All editorial, review, and advertising inquiries should be addressed to ronna.johnson@tufts.edu and ngrace@wooster.edu.

Inquiries concerning orders should be addressed to PaceUP@pace.edu.

CPSIA information can be obtained at www.ICGtesting.com
Printed in the USA
BVOW011538120612

292438BV00005B/2/P